THE SHORTER CATECHISM

Volume 1: Questions 1–38

G. I. Williamson

ILLUSTRATED BY

THOMAS TYSON

PRESBYTERIAN AND REFORMED PUBLISHING CO.
Phillipsburg, New Jersey

ISBN: 0-87552-539-3

Library of Congress Catalog Card No. 77-139855
Printed in the United States of America

To Doris

FOREWORD

This catechism study was written while the author was pastor of one of the Reformed Churches of New Zealand. The method of study was as follows: Students were expected to read each lesson carefully before class, and to write out their answers to the questions. Then, at the time of the week when the class met, these answers were recited and discussed. When a wrong—or inadequate—answer was given, the author did not immediately issue a definitive correction. Rather, members of the class were encouraged to evaluate, criticize, and attempt to formulate the right answer. In this way they learned to think out the implications of the doctrine being studied. The goal was to lead the class through discussion to a sharp discrimination between true and untrue, adequate and inadequate answers.

It will be noted that there are diagrams included in an appendix. These are not referred to at any predetermined point in the text. It is expected that the instructor will bring these into use whenever the discussion warrants, in order to help the students to grasp the interrelation of the doctrines being studied. It is the conviction of the author that there is a *system* of doctrine taught in the Bible. It is this system that this workbook aims to inculcate. These diagrams were helpful in the original instance. They were referred to again and again until they were thoroughly understood by the students.

If there is any value in this study—and in the illustrations that go with it—the "catechism kids" of theMangereReformed Church of Auckland deserve much of the credit. They were a never failing encouragement to the author as we worked through these lessons together.

G. I. W.

LESSON ONE

Question 1.   What is the chief end of man?

Answer: Man's chief end is to glorify God[1] and to enjoy Him forever.[2]

1. Whether therefore ye eat, or drink, or whatsoever ye do, do all to the glory of God (I Cor. 10:31). Thou art worthy, O Lord, to receive glory and honour and power: for thou hast created all things, and for thy pleasure they are and were created (Rev. 4:11).

2. Whom have I in heaven but thee? and there is none upon earth that I desire besides thee. My flesh and my heart faileth: but God is the strength of my heart, and my portion for ever (Ps. 73:25, 26).

According to the Catechism, there is a reason for the existence of human beings. And this reason cannot be found in man himself! This is so because God created man. God created man in His own image. And man, as originally created, was a true image of God because he was God-centered rather than self-centered. His one thought and desire, before sin ruined everything, was to serve God and to take delight in Him. When man (Adam) first sinned against God all was changed. Instead of thinking about how great and wonderful God is, he began to think about himself. He began to think of what it would be like if he (Adam) himself could be great, and of how he could enjoy himself!

Let us try to show the difference between these two situations. On the next page Figure A represents man (Adam) as originally created. It shows that all the activities of life were performed in the service and enjoyment of God. Figure B represents man (fallen) as we now find him in sin. It shows that all the activities of life are performed in the service and enjoyment of self!

It is quite true, of course, that there are people who do not live to glorify God and to enjoy Him who do not seem to belong to the description given in Figure B. They may devote themselves to various things which seem not to be self-centered. A man may devote himself to the service of his country, for example. Or perhaps a man will seek "the good of humanity." There have been those who have lived by the idea of "the greatest good for the

1

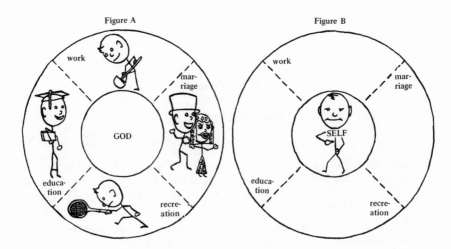

Figure A   Figure B

work   work

mar-   marriage   riage

GOD   SELF

educa-   education   tion

recre-   recreation   ation

greatest number (of people)." But, in reality, this too is really the same conception of life that we find in Figure B. It is the same because it is not *God*-centered, and it is *man*-centered. <u>The person who seeks the good of man as his chief end is really seeking his own good,</u> for the simple reason that he too is a man! So, it is only the Christian (the person who truly believes in the Lord Jesus Christ) who can glorify God and enjoy Him forever. And the first section of the Catechism will show how we can become God-centered people who glorify God and enjoy Him forever.

To "glorify God" does not mean "to *make* God glorious." God already is glorious. He has been glorious from all eternity, and nothing created by God can ever make Him more glorious than He already is. To "glorify God" must therefore be understood this way: it means to reflect God's glory. We see this in Psalm 19:1, "The heavens *declare* the glory of God; and the firmament *sheweth* his handywork." The beautiful world that God has created is something like a mirror. If you look into that "mirror" you can see the glory of God. The chief end of the heavens and the earth, then, is to declare or show forth the glory of God. But in the case of men there is this difference: we are invited to do this because we want to do it. The heavens cannot help but declare the glory of God. But we are given the wonderful privilege of doing it because we want to do it. That is what Jesus did when He was on earth in service to His Father. "I have glorified thee on the earth: I have finished the work which thou gavest me to do."

2

(John 17:4). He did what God wanted Him to do. He did it because He wanted to do it. In this way Jesus glorified God, and will enjoy Him forever!

Many people do not want to glorify God and enjoy Him forever. (In fact, none except those who come to repent of their sin and put their faith in Christ ever do.) Since there are many who do not want to glorify God, it may seem that the Catechism is incorrect when it says that "Man's chief end *is* to glorify God." But the Catechism is correct. Even if a person does not want to glorify God—even if a person does not want to serve God willingly—he still remains subject to God. "Hath not the potter power over the clay," says Paul, "of the same lump to make one vessel unto honour, and another to dishonour? What if God, willing to show his wrath, and to make his power known, endured with much longsuffering the vessels of wrath fitted to destruction: and that he might make known the riches of his glory on the vessels of mercy, which he had afore prepared unto glory" (Rom. 9:21-23). In other words, both the lost and the saved are instruments by which God's glory is revealed. By means of the one (those who are saved) God's mercy can be seen and praised. By means of the other (those who are lost) God's wrath and justice can be seen and honored. The difference is that in the case of those who are lost (who do not repent and believe in Christ) God causes them to glorify Him even though they do not enjoy it. But in the case of those who are saved they come to want to glorify God and they do enjoy Him forever.

When the Catechism speaks of "man's chief end" it must not be supposed that the true Christian life can be divided up into various departments or compartments separated the one from the other. It is true, of course, that the Christian may have other "ends" (goals, aims, purposes) in life other than what we call "religion." Worship alone, in other words, is not the whole of the Christian life, nor is "witnessing for Christ," or "Christian service," etc. Nor are we to suppose that if a person preaches the gospel he necessarily glorifies God. Many preachers preach false doctrine and do not glorify God. And many Christians do their daily work in the factory or place of business in such a way that they do glorify God! The true view is that when a person seeks to glorify God, he seeks at all times and in all activities alike to do that which is well pleasing in God's sight. Faithful work, and wholesome recreation, are just as much a part of glorifying God as is the worship of God on the Sabbath, or witnessing to an unbeliever. It is no doubt true that some things that we do are more important than other things. But the

3

true view of Christian discipleship is that which sees the whole of life as that which is to be consciously lived unto the honor of God, and in the service of His name!

Having said that all of life is to be God-centered (Fig. A), we must again emphasize the fact that no man can possibly live such a God-centered life until he is converted unto Christ. In order to know *how* we can glorify God and enjoy Him forever, we must learn the way of salvation taught in the Bible. We must learn "what man is to believe concerning God, and what duty God requires of man." To this we shall devote our attention in the Catechism questions which follow.

Questions:

1. What is meant by the word "chief" in the Catechism?
2. What is meant by the word "end" in the Catechism?
3. What is meant by the word "glorify"?
4. Why is man's chief end what the Catechism says that it is?
5. Man, as originally created, was ....-centered.
6. Man, as he became by sin, is ....-centered.
7. What do we mean by saying that the true Christian life is God-centered?
8. What would some people put in the center of Figure B rather than the word "self"?
9. Why is this really just as bad?
10. What does "glorify God" *not* mean?
11. What is the difference between the way in which the heavens glorify God, and the way in which man ought to glorify God?
12. Do the wicked glorify God? Explain.
13. Is it proper for a Christian to have other "ends" besides the end of glorifying God?
14. What departments of life ought to serve the glory of God?
15. Which is more to the glory of God: a person who preaches, or a man who works in a factory? Explain.

LESSON TWO

Question 2. What rule has God given to direct us how we may glorify and enjoy Him?

Answer: The Word of God which is contained in the Scriptures of the Old and New Testaments,[1] is the only rule to direct us how we may glorify and enjoy Him.[2]

1. All scripture is given by inspiration of God, and is profitable for doctrine, for reproof, for correction, for instruction in righteousness (II Tim. 3:16).

2. If any man shall add unto these things, God shall add unto him the plagues that are written in this book: and if any man shall take away from the words of the book of this prophecy, God shall take away his part out of the book of life . . . (Rev. 22:18, 19).

Strange as it may seem, Jesus once said that God has "hid . . . things from the wise and prudent, and . . . revealed them unto babes" (Luke 10:22). In other words, some of the most intelligent and best-educated people lack true wisdom. And some very simple people who are not well educated have true wisdom. The reason for this is that man, of himself, cannot really come to the knowledge of the truth. The more a man learns by his own effort (by the unaided power of his own mind), the more he faces the unknown. Just as a balloon, when it is blown up, expands in every direction, so does man's learning bring him face to face with the endless mystery of the wonderful works of God. For example, new and more powerful telescopes have been invented by men in order that they might study the secrets of the stars. But what has been the result? The result has been this: they now have many millions of new stars to study! This is one reason why scientific theory is constantly changing. For the more men discover, the more they also discover how much more there is that they do not know. Thus, because men cannot know *everything* (there is just too much!), they finally get discouraged and realize that they cannot really know *anything for sure.*

Now the reason for this is that God did not make man to know everything (or, for that matter, anything) by his own power. Only God knows every-

5

thing, and so, from the beginning, only God could give to man a sure knowledge of anything at all. From the beginning, this knowledge came to man in two ways. (1) The first way in which God revealed himself is what we call *natural revelation.* "The heavens declare the glory of God," says the Psalmist, "and the firmament sheweth his handywork" (Ps. 19:1). "The invisible things of him [God] from the creation of the world are clearly seen, being understood by the things that are made" (Rom. 1:20). (2) The second way in which God revealed himself is what we call *special revelation.* For even in paradise God spoke to Adam. Adam had God's word in addition to his works. Adam, by his study of nature, could know much. But he could not know all. He could not know, for example, what had not yet come to pass. In order to be sure of so "simple" a thing as eating fruit from a tree, it was necessary for him to interpret the "facts of nature" in the "light of God's Word."

When Adam sinned against God, he rejected God's word. He acted as if he did not need God to tell him what was right. Instead, he decided to try the so-called "scientific method" (that is, the "trial and error" method) of discovering truth. And from that time to this, Adam and all his posterity (except for those who come to salvation through Jesus Christ) have walked in darkness. This is not because of any "darkness" in God's revelation. The "light" of God still shines brightly in everything that God has made. But if man in the beginning (sinless Adam) could not understand the "light" of nature, without the "light" of God's word, how much more is this true for us! For the only way in which man can be saved from sin is revealed in the Bible alone. The revelation of God in nature is sufficient to leave men without excuse. It shows them the glory of the true God so that they *ought* to worship and serve Him. But it is only in the Bible that men actually can learn what they must believe (in order to be saved from sin) and do (in order to serve God once more).

But what does the Catechism mean when it says that "the word of God . . . is *contained* in the Scriptures of the Old and New Testaments"? By these words we are to understand that the very words which we find in the Bible are from God. However, in order to understand this clearly, we need to understand the wrong way in which these words (*contained in*) have been taken. We therefore give the illustration shown on the next page.

Since the time that this Catechism was written clever men have tried to use the same words ("contained in") with a meaning very different from what is intended by the Catechism. (1) The first (Fig. A) is called *Liberalism*

6

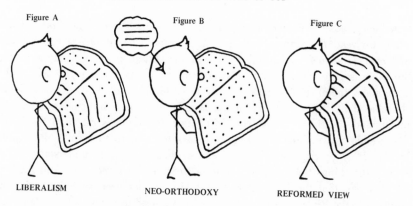

Figure A

Figure B

Figure C

LIBERALISM

NEO-ORTHODOXY

REFORMED VIEW

(or "the older modernism"). Those who hold this view believe that some parts of the Bible are the word of God (———), and that other parts are the word of man (-----). They believe that they can decide for themselves which part is true and which part is false. (2) The second (Fig. B) is called *Neo-orthodoxy* (or, the "new modernism"). This view is found today in many Protestant denominations. It is sometimes called "Barthianism" (after a famous theologian, Karl Barth). Men who believe this view say that the whole Bible is the fallible word of man. But they say that *when* people read these words of man (-----), God somehow uses these words so that through them they receive (in their own minds) the true word of God (———). Any part of the Bible can be the means by which the word of God comes to man, but it may be one part of the Bible that "speaks" to one man, and another part that "speaks" to another man. (3) The third (Fig. C) is the *Reformed* view. This is the view of the historic Christian faith. This is the view which is taught in the Catechism. Those who hold this view believe that the whole Bible (every single word) is the truth of God. No part is uninspired. And even when the Bible is read by an unbeliever it is still the word of God from cover to cover. In other words, the Bible *is* the word of God (———).

If the Bible is the word of God, the only rule to direct us how we may glorify God and enjoy Him forever, then three further things may be said. (1) First, we may say that the Bible is *infallible*. This means that everything that the Bible says is true. This does not mean that you can take every statement of the Bible as true apart from its context (or setting). For example, Psalm 53:1 says "there is no God"! But this is only part of the statement. The whole

7

statement reads: "The fool hath said in his heart, There is no God." Only when we read the whole Bible and understand what it *means* can we say that every statement is infallible. (2) In the second place, we may say that the Bible is *clear*. The Scriptures were written so that ordinary people could understand them. God speaks directly to children even (Eph. 6:1-3). Some churches deny this. They say that it is only the priests or scholars who can understand the Bible. (It is true, of course, that there is much in the Bible that we do not understand. Even scholars have more to learn.) But God, by His Holy Spirit, can and does lead ordinary people to understand quite clearly the things they need to know in order to be saved. (3) And finally, we may say that the Bible is *sufficient* (we do not need something else in addition to the Bible in order to know what we need to know). Many false religions deny this. The Roman Catholic Church says that we need tradition as well as the Bible. Mormons say that the *Book of Mormon* is needed as well as the Bible. Modernists tell us that we need "the findings of science" as well as the Bible. But Jesus said that the Bible is sufficient by itself (Rev. 22:18-20). The man who has the Bible, says the Bible itself, is "throughly furnished unto all good works (II Tim. 3:15-17). And what about the Creeds, Confessions, and Catechisms of Reformed churches? Well, we must always remember that these stand far below the Bible. They are not intended to be, and must not be treated as if they were, equal to the Bible in any way. We use them as convenient summaries of the teaching of the Bible. But we must never be content to just "believe the Catechism." We must always make sure that we personally prove the teaching of the Catechism by the Bible. Only then will our faith be acceptable and secure.

Questions:

1. What is meant by the word "contained" in the Catechism?
2. What is meant by the word "scriptures"?
3. What is meant by the word "rule"?
4. Are the educated and intelligent more certain to know God's truth than the uneducated and simple? Why?
5. Was man's knowledge originally supposed to come from nature alone? Why?
6. What are the two sources of "truth"?
7. What is the principle of the so-called "scientific method"?
8. What does natural revelation alone (by itself) now do for all men?

8

9. What does *Liberalism* mean when it says the Bible "contains" the Word of God?
10. What does *Neo-orthodoxy* mean by saying this?
11. What does *Reformed* Christianity mean by saying this?
12. What do we mean by saying the Bible is *infallible*?
13. What do we mean by saying it is *clear*? Who (for example) denies this?
14. What do we mean by saying it is *sufficient*? Who denies this?
15. If the Bible is what we say it is, why do we have the Catechisms?

LESSON THREE

Question 3. What do the Scriptures principally teach?

Answer: The Scriptures principally teach what man is to believe concerning God,[1] and what duty God requires of man.[2]

1. And many other signs truly did Jesus in the presence of his disciples, which are not written in this book: but these are written, that ye might believe that Jesus is the Christ, the Son of God; and that believing ye might have life through his name (John 20:30, 31).

2. He hath shewed thee, O man, what is good; and what doth the Lord require of thee, but to do justly, and to love mercy, and to walk humbly with thy God (Micah 6:8)?

There are many things that we cannot learn from the Bible. (1) For example, the Bible does not provide us with a complete history of the human race. This is not what the Bible was given for. So there are many things in history that we can learn only from other sources. (2) Neither does the Word of God provide us with technical information needed in the various sciences. There are no chemical formulae in the Scriptures. We do not find the principles of electronics. (3) As a matter of fact, the Bible does not even provide us with all the information that we might wish concerning Jesus Christ. We do not know very much about his boyhood, education, or home life. And we know nothing at all about his exact physical appearance. One could cite many other examples of what the Bible does not teach. For the Bible was not given in order to teach us everything. It was given to teach us "what man is to believe concerning God, and what duty God requires of man."

However, it is also important to remember that the Bible does have something to say about everything. And it has something to say that is very important. In fact, it is *so* important, that without what the Bible says we cannot really have a true understanding of anything. Let us illustrate in the following way:

In Fig. A we have a picture of man as he seeks to understand the world (and himself) without reference to God. This could be a modern scientist who

10

Figure A

Figure B

"Such as sit in darkness . . . because they rebelled against the words of God . . ."
Ps. 107:10, 11
". . . how great is that darkness!"
Matt. 6:23

"The entrance of thy words giveth light . . . thy word is a lamp unto my feet . . ."
Ps. 119:130
". . . and in thy light shall we see light."
Ps. 36:9

"believes" that the world just happens to be here because it evolved. In other words, at the very start of his study and investigation into the secrets of "nature," he just leaves God out completely. The same would apply to those who study history, or geography, or any other subject. For the Bible clearly teaches that everything in the universe is created. Everything is related to God, and it is this relationship to God which is the most important thing of all. Without this relationship being recognized, even "the greatest scientist" doesn't really understand the truth at all. In other words, when men do not begin their thinking with a recognition of the true God, they are in darkness. And because they are in darkness, they cannot really see the light that is in the world. In Fig. B we see a picture of a man who has come to see the light. It is the Bible that has given him this light (because the Holy Spirit has regenerated the heart so that God's Word is received and believed). But notice that we see two things here. First, we see how a knowledge of the Bible (given by the Holy Spirit) enables this man to believe in the true and living God. Secondly, we see how he is then able to understand his place in the world. He is able to understand that this is his Father's world, and that he must always seek the glory of God in everything that he does in this world. If this man is a scientist, he will study things in order to see more of God's wonderful creation. If he is a historian, he will study the history of the human race in order to understand the unfolding purpose of God. And so it is in every sphere. It is only by faith (what man is to believe concerning God) that we can walk uprightly (what duty God requires of man).

11

You will notice that this Catechism question introduces the basic outline of the rest of the Catechism. For in questions 4-38 we have a summary of what the Bible teaches us to believe concerning God. And in questions 39-107 (the law, the means of grace, and prayer) we have a summary of the duty which God requires of man. There are several things we need to observe at this point. (1) First, we need to notice that the Catechism places the greatest emphasis upon what we are to believe. This is important. It is commonly said today that what a person believes is really not so important. "Everyone has a right to believe whatever he wishes," say some. "Whatever a man believes is acceptable so long as he is sincere and decent toward others," say others. As Pope, the poet, has expressed it:

> For points of faith let senseless bigots fight
> His can't be wrong whose life is in the right.

It is true, of course, that no man should be forced by other men to believe anything he does not want to believe. But it is not true that it makes no difference what men believe. For "whosoever transgresseth, and abideth not in the doctrine of Christ, hath not God" (II John 9). Jesus said, to the woman at the well, "ye worship ye know not what: we know what we worship . . . and they that worship him must worship him in spirit and in truth" (John 4:24). Nothing could be more dangerous, then, than to imagine that one can really live a right life while having a wrong faith. "A good tree cannot bring forth evil fruit, neither can a corrupt tree bring forth good fruit" (Matt. 7:28). It is for this reason that the Catechism puts "what man is to believe concerning God" in first place. (2) Secondly, we need to notice that, when a man does actually have a true faith (if he really does believe what God commands him to believe), he must also do what God commands. In other words, there is no such thing as true faith unless it also results in right practice. "What doth it profit, my brethren," says James, "though a man say he hath faith, and have not works? can faith save him?" (James 2:14). No, says James, "faith, if it hath not works, is dead, being alone . . . [and] as the body without the spirit is dead, so faith without works is dead also" (2:17, 26). We see, then, that we would not have a true picture of the Christian life, if the Catechism did not emphasize both "what man is to believe concerning God" *and* "what duty God requires of man." There is such a thing as dead orthodoxy. It means that people profess the true doctrines of the Bible. They understand these doctrines in such a way as to be able to discuss them, and argue for them. But they

12

do not live the way God wants them to live. We must see how wrong this is. And we must see that the Catechism not only puts faith first, but also goes on to teach us that this faith is not a genuine saving faith unless it leads to right practice!

There is one other thing that we need to mention. The Bible speaks of the law (the ten commandments) as "our schoolmaster to bring us unto Christ, that we might be justified by faith" (Gal. 3:24). This means that a man cannot come to a true faith in Christ *as his savior* unless he first has come to realize his need. Or, in other words, it is only by the law that sinful men come to know that they are sinful. "For by the law is the knowledge of sin" (Rom. 3:20). So the question may be asked, "Why doesn't the Catechism *first* talk about the law, and then about the faith in Christ that we need in order to be saved?" In answer to this question we can say (1) that it would not be *wrong* if the Catechism first treated of law, and then of faith. God himself gave the law before he gave the Savior. (2) However, there are good reasons for not having the law treated in first place in the Catechism. What are these reasons? (a) First, there is the possibility that by putting the law first and then the faith in Christ second, the impression might be created that Christ is less important than the law. This would be very wrong. For Christ is greater than all. (b) Secondly, there is the possibility that careless readers could imagine that salvation comes by our doing what the law commands. Someone might say, "First you keep the law, and then Christ will accept you." And this would be completely wrong. For the Bible says that no man can ever be saved by (or because of) keeping the law. As a matter of fact no one (except Jesus) every really has kept the law of God the way God requires. (c) Thirdly, there is the possibility that by putting the law first, and then faith in Christ second, the impression might be created that we do not need the law of God after we believe in Christ! Someone might say, "Now that I have come to Christ, I do not need the law to tell me how to live." This, again, would be completely wrong. For the law is not only given by God to make us see that we need Christ as our savior, it is also given to show us how we ought to live for Christ after He is our savior. For "this is the love of God," says John, "that we keep his commandments" (I John 5:3).

In conclusion let us emphasize the fact that the Catechism firmly rejects the choice between Christianity as a doctrine and Christianity as a life. True Christianity is never one without the other. It is always both together: like the good tree and its fruit.

13

Questions:

1. What is meant by the word "principally" in the Catechism?
2. Are there things we cannot learn from the Bible? Give an example.
3. Name a subject about which the Bible says nothing whatsoever.
4. How much of the world does the man in Fig. A really understand correctly? Why?
5. Why does the man in Fig. B understand the world in a true sense?
6. Explain these words from the Bible: "in thy light shall we see light."
7. What are the two basic parts of the Catechism? Explain.
8. Upon what does the Catechism place first emphasis? Why?
9. Is true faith enough? Explain.
10. Would it be wrong if the Catechism treated the law before faith? Why?
11. What are some of the reasons in favor of treating faith before law?
12. What is the most important truth that we can learn from this Catechism question?

LESSON FOUR

Question 4.   What is God?

Answer: God is a Spirit,[1] infinite, eternal,[2] and unchangeable[3], in His
being wisdom, power, holiness, justice, goodness, and truth.[4]

1. God is a Spirit: and they that worship him must worship him in Spirit and in truth (John 4:24).

2. Before the mountains were brought forth, or ever thou hadst formed the earth and the world, even from everlasting to everlasting, thou art God (Ps. 90:2).

3. For I am the Lord, I change not (Mal. 3:6).

4. And God said unto Moses, I AM THAT I AM (Ex. 3:14). Great is our Lord . . . his *understanding* is infinite (Ps. 147:5). And they rest not day and night, saying, Holy, holy, holy, Lord God *Almighty* . . . (Rev. 4:8). Who shall not fear thee, O Lord, and glorify thy name? for thou only art *holy* . . . (Rev. 15:4). The Lord . . . *will by no means clear the guilty;* visiting the iniquity of the fathers upon the children. . . . The Lord God, merciful and gracious, longsuffering, and abundant in goodness and *truth* (Ex. 34:6, 7).

It was Jesus who said that "God is a Spirit" (John 4:24). The Catechism simply unfolds this text by defining the nature of that Spirit who is God. God is that Spirit who has certain attributes (or characteristics, qualities) which distinguish Him from all other beings in existence. It would not be correct, in other words, to say that "God is spirit." For God is not the only spirit. The Bible says that angels "are . . . all ministering spirits, sent forth to minister for them who shall be heirs of salvation" (Heb. 1:14). If we were just to say that "God is spirit," then we would fail to distinguish between God and other beings who are also spirits. (This would be a type of pantheism, which teaches that every spirit is a part of, or manifestation of, God!) But when we say that God is *a* Spirit we make clear the fact that He is distinct from other beings.

But what is "a Spirit"? The Bible says, "what man knoweth the things of

15

a man, save the spirit of man which is in him?" (I Cor. 2:11). Thinking, or knowing, is an activity of the spirit of a man. And the spirit of a man can be compared with God, since man was made in God's image. The spirit of a man is non-material: it cannot be seen, or felt, or weighed, or measured. We might say that "the spirit of a man" is like the thoughts of a man. But even when we have said all that we can safely say, we still have to confess that it is very hard to give a precise definition or description of a spirit. When we ask what a spirit is, we will have to confess that we cannot answer this question fully. There is an element of mystery here that we cannot overcome. But the important thing is that when we confess that God is a Spirit we *deny* that God has any material substance. As the child's Catechism puts it: God has *not* a body like men. God is invisible. No man has ever seen God, and no man ever will see God with his physical eyes (John 1:18; I John 4:12; etc.). It is a sin (against the second commandment) to try to make God visible by any kind of statue or picture (Ex. 20:4). And the prophet Isaiah asks the question: "to whom then will ye liken God? or what likeness will ye compare unto him?" (40:18). "Lift up your eyes on

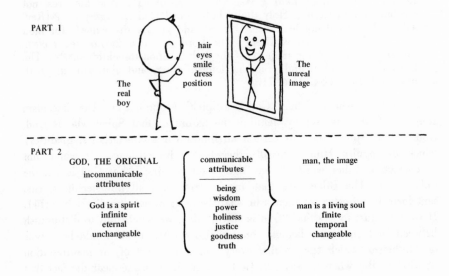

PART 1

hair
eyes
smile
dress
position

The
real
boy

The
unreal
image

PART 2

GOD, THE ORIGINAL
incommunicable
attributes

God is a spirit
infinite
eternal
unchangeable

communicable
attributes

being
wisdom
power
holiness
justice
goodness
truth

man, the image

man is a living soul
finite
temporal
changeable

16

high," he says, in answer to his own question, "and behold who hath created these things" (40:26).

The only way that we can "see" God, then, is *indirectly*. We can see Him only as we learn to see his "reflection" in the things that He has made. Again, we will try to illustrate this truth by means of a simple diagram (above).

Here, in part 1, we show our boy—let us call him "Shorty"—looking at his image in the mirror. We see quite clearly that two things are true. (1) First, we see that they (Shorty and his image) are *completely different*, since one is real or alive and the other is not. (2) Secondly, we see that they are *exactly alike*, since the image is a copy of Shorty in every detail.

It is much the same when we compare God with man who was made in His image. We see these same two things. (1) We see, first, that God is completely different from man. (2) And yet, secondly, we also see that man was made in the exact image of God. What we want to learn in this part of our study is to see how the Catechism question teaches us to think of God in both of these two ways. We show this, in part 2, without drawing any picture of God (since this is wrong). Now you notice that God has certain attributes (characteristics, qualities) which he does *not* "share" with man. God is infinite, but man is not infinite. God is eternal, but man is not eternal. God is unchangeable, but man is not unchangeable. These attributes we call *incommunicable*, because they belong to God alone. He does not give these to man but retains them for himself only. (This is somewhat like saying that Shorty does not give to his image in the mirror his own solid flesh, etc.) But we also notice that God has certain attributes which He *does* share with man. For he also gave man (before the fall) being, wisdom, power, etc. These attributes we call *communicable*, because God gives them to man in order that he might be like God. (This is something like the way Shorty gives his image in the mirror the same color hair and eyes, the same smile, etc.)

But now we come to the most difficult—and most important—point. We must realize that even when we speak of communicable attributes, we must remember that there is a difference between God and His image (man), even as there is also between Shorty and his image in the mirror. Both Shorty and his image have a smile. It is exactly the same smile, isn't it? No! When we stop and think about it, we can see that it isn't. For the smile on Shorty is a real smile, and the smile on the image is only the image of a smile! Shorty's smile is greater, just because it is real. So it is with the communicable attributes of God (wisdom, power, holiness, etc.). For God has all these in a far higher sense than man ever can. In other words, God's wisdom is always

17

infinite, eternal, and unchangeable wisdom. His power is infinite, eternal, and unchangeable, too. Whereas the wisdom of man, or the power of man, is always finite, temporal, and changeable. (This is like saying that Shorty's hair and eyes are always real, and the hair and eyes of his image are always unreal.)

But we must now briefly consider two questions that often arise when we grasp the teaching of the Catechism. (1) First, if God is a Spirit, how can the Bible speak of Him *as if* He had bodily parts? We read of "the hand of the Lord" (Josh. 4:24), "the eyes of the Lord" (I Kings 15:5), etc. In Exodus 24:10 we even read that Moses and others "saw the God of Israel: and there was under his feet as it were a paved work of a sapphire stone." No doubt some of the scripture texts which speak of God in such a way are simply meant to express in human terms what we could hardly understand in any other way. But many of these references concern the appearance of God in human form, and they are true descriptions of what people actually saw. But for this we know the reason. Just as angels (who are spirits) can manifest themselves by taking on a human appearance, so Christ likewise did the same during the Old Testament period of history (see Gen. 18:1-5, 16-25, etc.). These were what Calvin called "preludes to his future manifestation" as the God-man. And, of course, our Lord is God, and yet also (because He has a true human nature) does now have hands, feet, etc. (2) Secondly, if God is unchangeable, it is sometimes asked how the Bible can speak of Him *as if* He changed. In Genesis 6:6 we read: "and it repented the Lord that he had made man on the earth, and it grieved him at his heart." When a man repents, he changes his mind. But how can God repent if He is unchangeable? The answer is that when Scripture speaks like this of God, it always tells us first that it is man who has really changed. Man changes in his attitude or relationship to God. From this change in man himself there comes a change in God's manner of dealing with man. But the change is not really in God, it is only in man. God is always holy. But it is only when man sins against God that he comes under that holy anger which God always has against sin. The reason that God cannot change is that He cannot deny himself (see II Tim. 2:13). In other words, God is always determined in what He does by His own perfect nature. So, when a good creature becomes evil, God is necessarily grieved. He could not possibly be otherwise in view of His own unchangeable holiness.

Questions:

1. What is the meaning of the word "spirit"?

18

2. Define these terms: infinite, eternal, and unchangeable.
3. Why can't we say that God is spirit?
4. Are there other spirits besides God? Explain.
5. To what might we liken a spirit?
6. What does this Catechism answer teach us to deny as respects God?
7. What are the two kinds of attributes belonging to God?
8. Give a brief definition of each.
9. Are the communicable attributes the same in man as in God? Explain.
10. What does the Bible mean when it speaks of God as having hands, feet, etc.
11. What does the Bible mean when it speaks of God as repenting?
12. Be ready to discuss the diagram in this lesson, showing how it illustrates the teaching of the Catechism.

LESSON FIVE

Question 5.   Are there more Gods than one?

Answer: There is but one only,[1] the living and true God.

Question 6.   How many persons are there in the Godhead?

Answer: There are three persons in the Godhead: the Father, the Son, and the Holy Ghost,[2] and these three are one God, the same in substance, equal in power and glory.[3]

1. There is none other God but one (I Cor. 8:4).
2. Go ye therefore, and teach all nations, baptizing them in the name of the Father, and of the Son, and of the Holy Ghost (Matt. 28:19).
3. The grace of the Lord Jesus Christ, and the love of God, and the communion of the Holy Ghost, be with you all. Amen (II Cor. 13:14).

These two Catechism questions set before us the most important doctrine in the Christian faith. This is the doctrine of the Trinity. Someone has said that *all* error somehow traces back to a defective view of God. In any event, we cannot be *too* certain of this most important truth.

The doctrine of the Trinity can be expressed in three statements: (1) there is *one* God; (2) the Father *is* God, the Son *is* God, and the Holy Spirit *is* God; and (3) each of these three persons is *distinct* from the others. It will be observed that in the statement of this doctrine two seemingly contradictory truths are carefully safeguarded. These two truths are: the unity, and the plurality, of God. The unity is expressed in the fact that there is only one God. The plurality is expressed in the fact that there are three who are God. And it is often said that this makes no sense. Such false cults as Jehovah's Witnesses, for example, ridicule this doctrine of the Trinity. They say that those who believe this doctrine really believe in three Gods! Those who say this are not "trinitarians" but "unitarians." That is, they believe there is only one person (the Father, or Jehovah) who is God. They teach that Jesus is a *created* being (not self-existent, as the Father), and that the

Holy Spirit is merely a name for the power of God (not a person, as the Father). Unitarians (of which Jehovah's Witnesses are but one example) hold to the oneness of God, but deny that there are three distinct persons who *are* God. Polytheists (meaning: many + gods) believe that there are more than one being that may be called God. But they do not believe that these "gods" have *one* identical essence or substance of being. Mormons are polytheists.

Both of these—the unitarian and the polytheistic—seem simpler to understand than the doctrine of the Trinity. But let us not suppose that this is any argument *for* them, or *against* the historic Christian faith. For "my thoughts are not your thoughts," said the Lord, through His prophet Isaiah, "and my ways are not your ways" (55:8). In other words, we must always remember that the doctrine of the Trinity is *not* something that men have come to believe because it seemed reasonable to them. No, the only reason that we have for believing this doctrine is that Scripture allows no other view. Let us now consider some of these scripture truths which require us so to believe.

(1) *Scripture clearly teaches us that there is but one living and true God.* "The Lord is God and . . . there is none else" (I Kings 8:60). "For though there be that are called gods, whether in heaven or in earth, (as there be gods many, and lords many,) but to us there is but one God" (I Cor. 8:5, 6). "I am the first, and I am the last; and beside me there is no God" (Isa. 44:6). No truth is more emphatically or persistently taught in Scripture than this. There is but one God who really exists.

(2) *Scripture also teaches us clearly that not only the Father, but also the Son, and the Holy Ghost, are God.* Since no one disputes the fact that the Father is God, according to the Scriptures, we will cite only one scripture on this point. "No man hath seen God at any time, the only begotten Son, which is in the bosom of the Father, he hath declared him" (John 1:18). But Scripture also declares the Son to be God just as clearly. In Psalm 45:6 we read, concerning the Messiah, "thy throne, O *God*, is for ever and ever." And again, in Isaiah 9:6, 7, "unto us a son is given . . . and his name shall be called Wonderful, Counsellor, The mighty God, . . ." In the New Testament we read that "the Word was *God*" (John 1:1). And when "doubting" Thomas came to realize the truth, he came and fell before Jesus and said, "my Lord and my *God*" (John 20:28). Christ the Son is therefore, beyond any question, called God. But we also discover in the New Testament that Christ possesses the attributes of God. He has life in himself (John 1:4;

21

5:26)! He is everywhere present (Matt. 28:20). He was already existent in the beginning (John 1:1). We also note, in the New Testament record, that He performed the works of God. "All things were made by him" (John 1:3). He sustains all things (Col. 1:17; Heb. 1:3). "What things soever he [the Father] doeth, these also doeth the Son likewise" (John 5:19). And as we have seen (John 20:28), He was even worshiped as God. But, if the Son is thus called God, possesses the attributes of God, does the work of God, and even receives the worship that properly belongs to God, then what can we conclude except that He *is* God? And the same thing exactly may be said of the Holy Spirit. The evidence is of the same sort, and follows the same line. We will therefore give only one example of each type of evidence. In Acts 5:3, 4, the Holy Spirit is called God. "But Peter said, Ananias, why hath Satan filled thine heart to lie to the Holy Ghost . . . thou has not lied unto men, but unto God." In I Corinthians 2:10 we are told that the Holy Spirit has the attributes of God. "For the Spirit searcheth all things, yea, the deep things of God." The Holy Spirit also does the work that only God can do. "It is the Spirit that quickeneth" (that is, makes alive [John 6:63]). And to the Spirit belongs the worship and reverence that is God's. "All manner of sin and blasphemy shall be forgiven unto men," said Jesus, "but blasphemy against the Holy Ghost shall not be forgiven unto men" (Matt. 12:31). Again, we see that since the Holy Spirit is called God, and has the attributes of God, and does tthe work of God, and is to be worshiped as God, we can only conclude that the Holy Spirit is God.

(3) *Scripture also makes it clear that these three are distinct persons, and that they are equal* in power and glory. In early Church history there were two serious errors into which men fell as they tried to solve the mystery of the Trinity. (a) One of these was called "Modalism." It meant that God, according to this view, was one person, but that He "plays different parts" much like an actor who appears in a play, first as one character, and then (after a quick change into a different costume) another. They believed that while God played the part of the Father, there was no Son, and no Holy Spirit. And when He played the part of the Son, there was no Father, or Spirit. The reason that this was rejected by the Church is quite simple. It is because all three persons of the Godhead manifested themselves at the same time. "And *Jesus*, when he was baptized, went up straightway out of the water: and, lo, the heavens were opened unto him, and he saw *the Spirit* of God descending like a dove, and lighting upon him: and lo *a voice from*

22

heaven, saying, this is my beloved Son, in whom I am well pleased" (Matt. 3:16, 17). While Christ stood before men, the Spirit came down, while the Father spoke out of heaven. It could not, then, have been only one person playing three different parts, one after another. (b) Another was called "Monarchianism." This, of course, comes from the word "monarch," which refers to a king. And the basic idea was that only one of the three persons of the Godhead could really be "King." These people therefore said that God the Father was greater than the Son or the Holy Spirit. And they did not believe that the three persons were equal in power and in glory. It is possible to make this teaching seem to agree with Scripture. For Christ did say, "my Father is greater than I" (John 14:28). If we look only at texts such as these, we can begin to feel that there is a truth in this old view. But when we read such texts as Philippians 2:6 we can see why the Church rejected this error. For Christ, "being in the form of God, thought it not robbery to be equal with God." In respect of His eternal divine nature Christ *is* equal with the Father. It is only in respect of His human nature, and because He took such humiliation upon himself, that He can say "my Father is greater than I." Remembering this, we will not be attracted by this ancient error.

By the evidence of Scripture, then, we are driven to the doctrine of the Trinity—one God—three who are God—three who are distinct. And it is interesting that we have scripture statements that really do not make sense except in the light of the formulation of the Catechism. Christ said to baptize "in the *name* of the Father, and of the Son, and of the Holy Ghost" (Matt. 28:19). He did not say *"names,"* and so could only have referred to one being. Yet observe again: He did not say "of the Father, Son, and Holy Ghost," as if they were merely synonymous terms (like: me, myself, and I). No, He carefully distinguishes between these three as having each, His own identity and personality, that is "of the Father, and of the Son, and of the Holy Ghost." And this is the doctrine of the Trinity. It is true, of course, that the doctrine is fully revealed only when we take into account the whole teaching of Scripture. Yet it is interesting to observe that even from the beginning of divine revelation there is always an equal emphasis upon the two foundation truths contained in the doctrine of the Trinity. There is an equal emphasis upon the fact that God is a unity (one God) and a plurality (more than one person). "And *God* said, Let *us* make man in *our* image," we read, "so *God* created man in *his* own image . . ." (Gen. 1:26, 27). Here is a mystery that remained locked, until the key

23

was given in the full New Testament revealing of the Tri-une being of God.

Questions:

1. State the three essential truths that make up the doctrine of the Trinity.
2. What does "Godhead" mean?
3. What does "substance" mean?
4. What do unitarians believe? What modern cult is unitarian?
5. What do polytheists believe? What modern cult is polytheist?
6. Is the doctrine of the Trinity easy to understand? If not, then why do we believe it?
7. Cite a text of Scripture proving that there is only one God.
8. What four things which properly belong to God only, also can be proved from Scripture to belong to Christ and the Holy Spirit?
9. Give an example of each of these as respects the person of Christ.
10. Give an example of each of these as respects the person of the Holy Ghost.
11. What did "Modalism" teach? What scripture disproves this error?
12. What did "Monarchianism" teach?
13. What scripture could "Monarchianists" try to use to their advantage?
14. What answer could be given against this attempt?
15. Why does Matthew 28:19 require belief in the doctrine of the Trinity?
16. Is the doctrine of the Trinity taught in the Old Testament? Explain.

LESSON SIX

Question 7. What are the decrees of God?

Answer: The decrees of God are His eternal purpose according to the counsel of His will, whereby, for His own glory, He hath fore-ordained whatsoever comes to pass.[1]

1. According as he hath chosen us in him before the foundation of the world . . . being predestinated according to the purpose of him who worketh all things after the counsel of his own will (Eph. 1:4, 11).

The Bible says that God "worketh *all* things after the counsel of his own will" (Eph. 1:11). In other words, what we see happening in this world is not just a matter of chance or accident. Things do not just work out the way they do for no reason at all. No, there is a reason for everything. And the ultimate reason for everything is the great plan of God. "For of him, and through him, and to him, are all things: to whom be glory for ever." says the Scripture (Rom. 11:36). Sometimes we do not realize that God has planned everything that happens. But the Bible says that the Lord declares "the end from the beginning . . . saying my counsel shall stand, and I will do all my pleasure" (Isa. 46:10). As for man, says Job, "his days are determined, the number of his months are with thee, thou hast appointed his bounds that he cannot pass" (Job 14:5). For "the Lord hath made all things for himself, yea, even the wicked for the day of evil" (Prov. 16:4).

In order to illustrate this truth, let us try to show a human parallel to the great plan of God (see next page).

Here we see our friend Shorty finishing the plan for his house. Even before the foundation is laid, he has worked out just how it is to be done. And when the time comes to actually build the house, those who build it will have to follow this plan. Everything will have to be done according to this "blueprint." This is only a weak human comparison to the great plan of God, of course, but it does illustrate a real parallel. For just as Shorty plans everything that goes into his house, so God plans everything that happens

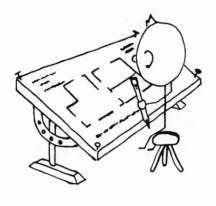

in the world. He has foreordained whatsoever comes to pass.

Having said this, we must also point out certain ways in which God's plan is not like the plans that people make. (1) One of these is that *God's plan is eternal.* In other words, if we were to ask, When did God work out this great plan of His?, the answer would be this: this plan is something that God has always had! He has had this plan forever! With human plans it is different. First there is a time when we do not have a plan worked out. Then there is the work of figuring out what seems to be the best. Finally we arrive at a suitable plan. But with God it is not so. For "the counsel of the Lord standeth for ever, the thoughts of his heart to all generations" (Ps. 33:11). God does not plan from day to day, as we do. Nor does He ever change His plan. He is infinite, eternal, and unchangeable. So His purpose —his plan—has always been in God's mind, and has never been changed, and never will be changed the least bit. That is why the Catechism says that God's "eternal purpose" is according to "the counsel of his will." When we make our plans we usually do so after consulting with others. We want the advice of others who may have more wisdom than we have. But God does not need this. He already knows everything. No one has wisdom that He does not have. There is nothing that He has not foreseen. Therefore, God did not make His plan by any process of consultation with others. He consulted only himself—so to speak—in order to make His plan agreeable with His own holy will. "O the depth of the riches both of the wisdom and knowledge of God: how unsearchable are his judgments, and his ways past finding out. For who hath known the mind of the Lord? or who hath been his counsellor?" (Rom. 11:33, 34).

(2) Another difference between the plan of God, and the plans that people make, is the fact that God's plan is *absolute.* That is, *nothing happens— nothing whatsoever—that God has not planned.* When a human makes a plan for a house, he has (by that plan) a *measure* of control over what happens. But this plan does not determine everything. It does not cover every detail, such as the exact number of nails to be used in building the house. Nor

26

does it determine before just how many days it will take to build the house. But God's plan does determine absolutely everything. It even includes two kinds of events or happenings in the world that people often think of as outside of God's control. (a) There are what we call "chance" or "accidental" events. When people gamble with dice or play cards they imagine that no one knows how things will turn out. They think that they have a "chance" to win. But the Bible says "the lot is cast into the lap; but the *whole* disposing thereof is of the Lord" (Prov. 16:33). In the book of Kings (II Kings 22) we read of King Ahab, who "took a chance" by going into battle against the warning of the Lord. We also read (vs. 34) of a Syrian soldier who shot an arrow into the air without aiming at any particular target. But *that* was the arrow that killed the King. All things are determined by the Lord. And so far as God's plan is concerned there are no "accidents"—no events that come as a surprise to God, or upset His plans. (b) But what about man's "free will," it may be asked? Are we to believe that even the choices that men make—whether for good or evil—are already predetermined by God? Yes, that is what the Scriptures teach us. For the Bible tells us that every decision made by every man—whether a believer or an unbeliever—is already planned by God from all eternity. Take, for example, what the Bible says about the evil deeds of those who killed the Lord Jesus. "Him, being delivered by the determinate counsel and foreknowledge of God," we read, "ye have taken, and by wicked hands have crucified and slain" (Acts 2:23). So, even though wicked men acted against God, they were still doing what He had planned! They may think that they are upsetting God's plan, but they are only fulfilling it. And if this be true of the unbelievers, how much more of the believers. For "we are his workmanship, created in Christ Jesus unto good works, which God hath before ordained that we should walk in them" (Eph. 2:10). Even the most important choice that a man can ever make—the choice to believe in Christ—is foreordained of God. When Paul preached at Lystra "as many as were ordained to eternal life believed" (Acts 13:48). So again we say it: nothing whatsoever is outside God's plan. His plan is absolute. It includes everything that happens.

(3) For what reason did God make this perfect and all-inclusive plan? The Catechism says it was "for His own glory!" This does not mean that by doing this God made himself more glorious than He was before. (Remember, there is no before or after in God.) It simply means that God does not explain what He does by giving us a reason that "goes beyond himself." God is the Alpha and Omega, the beginning and the end, from whom, by

whom, and for whom are all things. And so the reason for what God has planned can only be His own good pleasure, and the honor and praise that He would bring upon himself. "Thou art worthy, O Lord, to receive glory, and honor, and power: for thou hast created all things, and for thy pleasure they are and were created" (Rev. 4:11). If a human person were to do things because they were self-pleasing, and self-glorifying, we would consider such a one to be intolerably conceited. But it is *right* for God to do this, for the very same reason that it is *wrong* for a human person to do so. It is wrong for a human being because it would mean a practical denial of his being what he is (a mere creature). For God *not* to do so would also be a denial of His being (for He is the only true God, and of infinitely more worth than all that exists besides Him). God cannot deny himself. Since He *is* supreme, He must (to be true to himself) do His own good pleasure always, and seek His own glory above all.

Finally, let us observe that certain false inferences must not be drawn from the fact that "God has foreordained whatsoever comes to pass." (1) It is not true, for one thing, that God is the author of sin. This is difficult to understand. For, if we once say that God has planned everything, we cannot leave sin out. God has planned sin too, and if God has planned sin, it would almost *seem* that God must be the author of it. But here is one of the many places in which we must accept the Scripture, instead of follow what seems reasonable to us. And the Bible says that God is not the author of sin. God created angels and men. But they were good when God first made them. Somehow (and we do not know how) sin arose in these creatures. Satan is the real author of sin. God's plan included this, of course, but not in such a way as to make God the author of sin. (2) For another thing, we cannot say that human persons are treated as "pawns" on a chessboard. It is true, indeed, that God has already determined the destiny of every man. Some will be saved, as God has appointed. And some will be lost, as God has decreed. Some men, says Jude, "were before of old ordained to this condemnation" (v. 4); but "God hath not appointed us to wrath," says Paul, "but to obtain salvation" (I Thess. 5:9). But the Bible clearly teaches that those who are finally lost do not really want to be saved. They are lost because of their own choice. For the decree of God does not in any way weaken or destroy the responsibility of people.

Questions:

1. What does "decree" mean? And "counsel"? And "foreordained"?

28

2. What does the plan of God include?
3. What item in the illustration is *like* the "decrees" of God?
4. What are some of the differences between our human plans and the great plan of God?
5. Who gave God advice when He worked out His plan? Why?
6. What two kinds of events or happenings do people often think of as being "outside" God's control? Prove that they are included in His plan.
7. When did God make His plan?
8. For what reason did God make His plan?
9. Does this not mean that God is self-centered? If so, why is this not wrong for God, and yet wrong for man?
10. What are the two (common) false inferences often drawn from this doctrine of the "decrees"?
11. Answer both of these false inferences.

LESSON SEVEN

Question 8. How does God execute His decrees?

Answer: God executeth His decrees in the works of creation and providence.

Question 9. What is the work of creation?

Answer: The work of creation is God's making all things of nothing,[1] by the word of His power,[2] in the space of six days, and all very good.[3]

1. In the beginning God created the heaven and the earth (Gen. 1:1).

2. Through faith we understand that the worlds were framed by the word of God; so that things which are seen were not made of things which do appear (Heb. 11:3).

3. And God saw every thing that he had made, and behold, it was very good. And the evening and the morning were the sixth day (Gen. 1:31).

In our last lesson we considered the decrees of God. We saw, in other words, that God has planned everything. This we tried to illustrate by showing how we too plan things before we do them. Thus, in Illustration 5, we saw Shorty making up the plan for his house. Before there ever was a house the plan was complete. And now, in Illustration 6 (on the next page) we illustrate the way in which Shorty carries out his plan.

In the first picture, we see Shorty building the house which he had planned. This suggests the work of creation. In the second picture we see him taking care of his house after it has been completed. This suggests the work of providence. In the remainder of this lesson, and in the next, we will consider the work of creation. Then we will go on to deal with the work of providence in later lessons.

When the Catechism says that God made "all things of nothing, by the word of his power, in the space of six days," it says something that is truly stupendous. And we must not allow our illustration to suggest that God's

30

work of creation is the same as the human activity of building. For there are two very great differences. (1) For one thing, we note that when man builds—or "makes"—something, he always has to use materials that are already at hand. He uses wood, and bricks, and cement, etc. But when God created the world He did not use any existing materials. For "the things which are seen were not made of things which do appear" (Heb. 11:3). God "spake, and it was done; he commanded, and it stood fast" (Ps. 33:9). This is what we call "creation out of nothing." (2) For another thing, we observe that the work of building—or "making"— is a time-consuming process. Whereas, with the Lord "one day is . . . as a thousand years, and a thousand years as one day" (II Pet. 3:8). So we simply believe, on the authority of the Bible, that God created the whole universe in the space of six days. And we must not allow ourselves to be carried away from this conviction by the theories of modern science.

The theory of modern science, which is very powerful today, is directly against this teaching of the Catechism. According to the theory of evolution, the world (or, universe) as we now see it, is the result of a very slow and steady development. And people who believe that God created the world in a short space of six days are usually considered foolish. But the Bible itself reminds us, "by faith we understand that the worlds were framed by word of God" (Heb. 11:3). If we try to understand how the world came to be what it is, through our own human wisdom, it is natural that we should follow the path of unbelieving science. *We* do not see a tree growing up in one day. *We* do not see men created as adults (as Adam and Eve were). And so, because it takes time now for trees to grow up, and for people to

31

grow to be adults, we may find it hard to imagine that such things could happen all at once. But when we begin to reason this way what we really are doing is this: We are making the mistake of thinking that God was—in the work of creation—subject to limitations that we ourselves experience. The truth is that there is no good reason to think this way. If we think more accurately (that is, biblically), we will understand that *time* is not something that was "already there" when God began to create. Time does not have independent existence. *Only* God exists without being created. And time too is a created thing. It was not just "there" when God began to create the world.

We can best illustrate what we mean by asking a question: How much space did God "use up" in creating space? The answer, of course, is that God did not use space to create space. He created space out of nothing. So again, when we ask how much time God used up in creating our system of time (in other words, our solar system, for that is what measures our time), the answer can only be: no time at all. He created time (like all other things) out of nothing. Let us therefore be content to simply *believe* (Heb. 11:3) that God spoke and it was done, that He commanded and it stood fast. Let us believe that this stupendous work of creation was done with such divine power that it was completed in six days. This is surely the impression that we get—and that we are intended to get—from reading the first chapter of Genesis. To say that the Lord has made a "short" work is but another way of saying that He is God, and that He can do all His holy will. The choice is a clear one. The basic thought in all unbelieving science is this: "all things continue as they were from the beginning" (II Pet. 3:4). In other words, the unbelieving scientist observes how things are happening *now,* and then he concludes that this is the only way that things ever have happened. But the basic thought in Christian faith is that the Bible tells us the truth when it tells us about things that are not happening now. We think, for example, of the miracles of Christ. At the wedding feast at Cana (John 2:1-11) Jesus made wine—the best wine—by an instantaneous act of divine power. It was just *like* wine that would ordinarily take even a hundred years to make through usual processes. This, we believe, is a true indication of God's power in creation. If the Lord could create wine in an instant, why should we not believe also that He created the universe in six days?

Finally, we observe that the Catechism teaches that the creation was "all very good" when it "came from the hand of God." In the Bible itself we read (Gen. 1:12, 18, 25, etc.), "behold, it was very good." What this means is not only plainly evident but also extremely important. It means that evil

32

does not have its origin in the inherent nature of things, but only in the moral perversion of beings who abuse them. Take wine, for example. Wine is a created thing. Jesus himself created wine. The Bible therefore declares that it is good. We are told in Scripture that "wine . . . maketh glad the heart of man" just as the oil makes "his face to shine, and bread gives strength to his heart" (Ps. 104:15). Drunkenness is called a sin in the Bible. But it is not said in the Bible that wine is to blame for this sin. No, it is rather caused entirely by the sinfulness of man. It is not what goes into the mouth of the sinner that corrupts him, but only what comes out of his heart (Mark 7:15). "For *every* creature [created thing] is good, and nothing to be refused, if it be received with thanksgiving" (I Tim. 4:4). This teaching is extremely important because there has always been the tendency in the history of the Church to seek to locate the cause of human sin outside of man himself, and therefore (since there is hardly any other choice) in material things in the world. Thus, when a material thing is frequently abused, it is tempting to place the blame for the sin on this "thing" rather than on the man who misuses it. Then it is easy to say: "touch not, taste not, handle not . . . after the commandments and doctrines of men" (Col. 2:21, 22). Once this fundamental error (that evil resides in material things) is submitted to, there is the beginning of a bondage that is harmful in the extreme. One thing after another becomes "taboo" and more and more uncertainty enters the heart. How very important it is, then, to remember that "there is nothing from without a man, that entering into him can defile him" (Mark 7:15). And it is this wonderful doctrine of divine creation that protects us from this danger.

Questions:

1. In Illustration 6, with what is God's work of creation compared?
2. In Illustration 6, with what is God's work of providence compared?
3. What two things in God's work of creation are *not* to be compared with the activity of humans?
4. What does the theory of modern science teach as to the origin of the world?
5. Why does this theory "seem" reasonable to unbelieving men?
6. What is the one basic error in this kind of thinking?
7. How much "time" did it take God to create the world? Explain.
8. How do the miracles of Christ help us to "understand" the creation of the world?

9. Why is it important to believe that when God created the world all things were "very good"?
10. What is the reason that this is so often forgotten?
11. What happens when men forget this?
12. What text of the Bible can be cited to refute the teaching that material things are evil?
13. Be ready to explain orally how pictures 5 and 6 illustrate God's decree, and His works of creation and providence.

LESSON EIGHT

Question 10. How did God create man?

Answer: God created man male and female, after His own image,[1] in knowledge, righteousness, and holiness,[2] with dominion over the creatures.[3]

1. So God created man in his own image, in the image of God created he him: male and female created he them. (Gen. 1:27).

2. And have put on the new man, which is renewed in knowledge after the image of him that created him (Col. 3:10). And that ye put on the new man, which after God is created in righteousness and true holiness (Eph. 4:24).

3. And God blessed them, and God said unto them, be fruitful, and multiply, and replenish the earth, and subdue it: and have dominion over the fish of the sea, and over the fowl of the air, and over every living thing that moveth upon the earth (Gen. 1:28).

In our previous lesson we saw that God created all things. This lesson concerns itself with the creation of man in particular. And the reason for this special interest in man is the fact that Scripture teaches us that all things were made so as to "fit together," or "work out their purpose and meaning" under the headship of man. To use an illustration, creation without man would have been like a great ship without a captain, or like a great army without a leader. It was man alone among all the creatures of God who was made in God's own image. It was to man alone that God spoke these words, "Be fruitful, and multiply, and replenish the earth, and subdue it: and have dominion over the fish of the sea, and over the fowl of the air, and over every living thing that moveth upon the earth" (Gen. 1:28).

It is sometimes said, even by Christians, that this truth of man's headship over creation can be harmonized with the theory of evolution. Those who try to do this are often called theistic evolutionists. They would agree with the teaching of evolution to a great extent, as a description of the process of development that has taken place in the world. First came the one-celled animals, and then the more complex, etc. But they believe that this happened because God is "behind" it all, controlling the various stages of development. Theistic evolutionists, for example, could believe that the body of man did indeed descend from the apes. But they would say that God created something new at a given point, namely, the human soul or spirit, and only when this happened did "man" really begin to exist as the bearer of the divine image. What are we to think of this doctrine of theistic evolution (evolution as the method of God's creation)? (1) For one thing, it is not in accord with Genesis 2:7, which says that "the Lord formed man of the dust of the ground, and breathed into his nostrils the breath of life; and man became a living soul." The animals, to which God had already given life, could hardly be called "the dust of the ground." If God had made man by adding something to an already living creature, why would God need to give him "the breath of life"? Genesis 2:7 clearly teaches that man did not evolve. (2) For another thing, it is nowhere stated in the Bible that we are to think of the *body* of man as a "beastly" thing, while we think of the *soul* as something "angelic." It is true, of course, that man is dichotomous (that is, of a twofold nature), having a physical body and a non-material spirit, or soul. Our Lord himself said, "fear not them which kill the body, but are not able to kill the soul: but rather fear him which is able to destroy both soul and body in hell" (Matt. 10:28). But when it is said that the body of man evolved from lower forms of life, and that the soul only was immediately created by God, there is really present (whether consciously or not) the thought that somehow the soul of man is better than the body, and that the one comes from God in a more fundamental sense than the other. And this is not what the Bible teaches. This is why the Christian faith—unlike the false religions—holds forth the hope of the resurrection of the body, and not merely the survival of the soul after death! God created the whole man, and it is the whole man that will be either saved by the Lord Jesus Christ, or condemned by God at the last day.

But what is meant by saying that man was created in the image of God? This we believe to be best understood if we think of man as he was originally created in the following way:

(1) The Catechism says that God created man after His own image in *knowledge*. This means that Adam, while he was without sin, was able to understand God's revelation of himself in the world. When "Adam gave names to all cattle, and to the fowl of the air, and to every beast of the field" (Gen. 2:20), he was doing something more than merely "thinking up names."

36

Figure A

PROPHET
(Knowledge)
". . . in thy light shall we see light."
Ps. 36:9b

Figure B

PRIEST
(Holiness)
"Let your heart therefore be perfect"
I Kings 8:61a

Names were really true descriptions of the things that were named. When Adam named his wife Eve (which means "life-giving"), he did so because "she was the mother of all living" (Gen. 3:20). When Adam studied the animals too, and gave them names, he showed himself able to grasp—and to express—the true nature of things. In other words, Adam (while yet without sin) was a prophet in the highest sense. For a prophet is one who can *see* the truth of God (a prophet was often called a "seer") and speak the same for the benefit of others.

(2) The Catechism also says that God created man after His own image in *holiness*. This means that Adam, while he was without sin, was wholly consecrated to God. In the Old Testament we find this concept carefully developed in the system of worship revealed by God through Moses. There was the high priest, the tabernacle, and the various offerings. There were the divine ceremonies. And the basic idea of holiness was always prominent. Holiness meant "being set apart to the Lord." In Adam's case this was not a matter of ceremonies, or sacrifices. It was, in his case, a matter of heart devotion. He was holy because he found his supreme delight in the Lord. Far from being afraid (before he sinned), Adam felt at peace in the presence of God. He was "set apart" unto the Lord in all things, by a willing desire. He was, in this sense, truly a priest.

(3) The Catechism finally states that God created man after His own image

Figure C

KING
(Righteousness)
"... this is the way, walk ye in it ..."
Isa. 30:21

in *righteousness*. Righteousness is but another name for obedience to God. He who does what God will have him do, does that which is righteous. So it is quite proper to say that Adam, before he sinned, was a king. A king is someone who rules. Adam ruled over all the world that God had placed under his dominion. Because he *knew* the Lord's will (as a prophet), and *desired* to serve Him only (as a priest), he was also *able* to do the works of righteousness as king of creation. Thus we see that it is not really accurate to speak of the image of God *in* man. It is rather proper to speak of man himself as the very image of God. The image of God was not something in man, or some part of man (the soul). No, man himself—thinking as a prophet, feeling as a priest, and acting as a king—was the image of God.

We do well to keep this in mind as we study the remainder of the Catechism. For it is only with a proper understanding of man as the image of God at creation, that we can come to understand many other doctrines of the Christian faith. Let us briefly cite some examples. (1) The doctrine of *man's total depravity* can be understood only if we first grasp the meaning of man's creation in the divine image. It was the whole man that fell in Adam's first transgression, and it is the whole man who is now corrupt in every part. (2) Again, it is in the light of this teaching that we can best understand *the saving work of Christ*. The Old Testament unfolds the promise of the Savior, to be sent into the world by the Father, in terms of the prophets, priests, and kings of the biblical history. Jesus, in order to save His people from their sins, had to be the perfect prophet, priest, and king. If we keep what we have learned in this lesson firmly in mind, we will better understand why this was so. (3) Another doctrine that we can better understand, if we keep this lesson firmly in mind, is the *conversion* of the sinner to Christ. We will see why it is that true conversion involves knowledge, feeling, and will. (4) And finally, it is in the light of this teaching that we can understand *the marks of a true Church* to be what they are. The true Church of Christ is not a

38

building, it is an organism—a body of people—who belong to the Lord. It is, in other words, a company of those who have been converted to true knowledge, righteousness, and holiness. And, as we shall see, this is why the marks of the true Church must be the faithful preaching of the Word of God, the true administration of the sacraments, and the faithful exercise of Church discipline. In these things we see the glorious fulfillment of Christ's ministry as prophet, priest, and king. And by these we also see His people themselves becoming partakers of these things.

Questions:

1. Why does the Catechism devote another question (besides question 9) to the doctrine of creation (this time—the creation of man)?
2. What do theistic evolutionists believe about the origin of man?
3. What reasons can you give for rejecting theistic evolution?
4. Does man have a twofold nature (body and soul)? Prove.
5. Which (body or soul) is the "highest" or best?
6. In Illustrations 7a, 7b, and 7c, what is Shorty doing that illustrates the lesson?
7. In your own words tell briefly what you think a prophet should be. A priest. A king.
8. Which of these is correct: "The image of God is in man," or, "Man is the image of God," or, "The soul contains the image of God." Why did you choose the one you did?
9. What other doctrines can better be understood in the light of this lesson? Be ready to explain why, in one instance, in class.

LESSON NINE

Question 11. What are God's works of providence?

Answer: God's works of providence are, His most holy,[1] wise,[2] and powerful preserving and governing[3] all His creatures, and all their actions.[4]

1. The Lord is righteous in all his ways, and holy in all his works (Ps. 145:17).

2. This also cometh from the Lord of hosts, which is wonderful in counsel, and excellent in working (Isa. 28:29).

3. Upholding all things by the word of his power (Heb. 1:3). His kingdom ruleth over all (Ps. 103:19).

4. Are not two sparrows sold for a farthing? and one of them shall not fall upon the ground without your Father (Matt. 10:29).

God executes His decrees not only in the work of creation, but also in the works of providence. And, according to the Catechism, God's providential activity is of two kinds: (1) He *preserves*, and (2) He *governs*. To illustrate the teaching of the Catechism, let us think of Shorty in two situations:

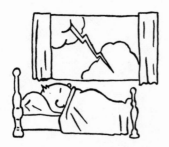

"Thou shalt not be afraid for the terror by night"

Ps. 91:5

"A thousand shall fall at thy side . . . but it shall not come nigh thee."

Ps. 91:7

40

In our first illustration we see Shorty peacefully sleeping in the midst of a storm. This, of course, is just what a Christian ought to do. For he should realize that it is God who preserves and keeps us. People often forget this. They talk about the "laws of nature," and the "discoveries of modern science." They seem to forget that it is really God who is "upholding all things by the word of his power" (Heb. 1:3). And it is easy for us, as Christians, also to forget that God is "not far from every one of us: for in him we live, and move, and have our being" (Acts 17:27, 28). But the truth is that all things would instantly pass away if God did not uphold them. "Thou preservest them all," says Nehemiah (9:6). "By him all things consist," says the Apostle (Col. 1:17). Even Satan could not exist for one moment if God did not sustain him in his existence (but, of course, *not* in his wickedness) by the word of His power!

In our second illustration we see Shorty in the midst of many dangers of battle. Yet, under the picture we quote a portion of Psalm 91, which says, "a thousand shall fall at thy side, and ten thousand at thy right hand; but it shall not come nigh thee" (v. 7). What we are trying to show, in this illustration, is that God governs "all creatures, actions, and things from the greatest to the least" (as we read in the Westminster Confession, V, i). This does not mean that no one will die in battle. What it means is that God is able to spare the life of His servant if He pleases to do so. He is able to so direct and control everything that happens in that situation that His servant will be safe. It is this confidence, and this only, that enables a Christian to stand in many dangerous places without being overcome by fear. "God is our refuge and strength, a very present help in trouble. Therefore will not we fear, though the earth be removed, and though the mountains be carried into the midst of the sea" (Ps. 46:1, 2).

But let us consider what the Bible teaches in a more detailed way, about God's providential works. (1) Consider, for one thing, what Scripture says about *the complete control of* (what we call) *nature*. He "maketh his sun to rise on the evil and on the good and sendeth rain on the just and the unjust" (Matt. 5:45). "He causeth the grass to grow for the cattle, and herb for the service of man; that he may bring forth food out of the earth" (Ps. 104:14). And "by the breath of God frost is given . . . also by watering he wearieth the thick cloud . . . and it is turned round about by his counsels: that they may do whatsoever he commandeth them upon the face of the world in the earth" (Job 37:10, 12). To *us* it often seems that all these things happen "by chance," or in a "mechanical" way. But the Bible says that God

41

exercises complete control of them. (2) Observe also what the Bible says about *the nations of men* that dwell on the earth. How often it seems to us that they are out of control. They seem to do such unexpected things, such as suddenly going to war. But the Bible says that "the Most High ruleth in the kingdom of men" (Dan. 4:25). "He changeth the times and the seasons; he removeth kings and setteth up kings" (Dan. 2:21). So it is not by any accident that things work out the way they do. It is not "chance" or "fate" that makes "the wheel of human history" turn. It is the Lord, who has "determined the times before appointed" and it is He who rules "the bounds of their habitation" (Acts 17:26). (3) And we even see, in the Bible, that God exercises complete control over *every single individual* in the world. "The Lord killeth and maketh alive: He bringeth low and lifteth up. He raiseth up the poor out of the dunghill, to set them among princes, and to make them inherit the throne of glory: for the pillars of the earth are the Lord's, and he hath set the world upon them" (I Sam. 2:6-8). Just as the little sparrow depends upon the providence of God in life and death, so man too depends upon God in all things. The very hairs of his head are numbered by the Lord, as is the number of the days of his life on this earth. (4) Finally, we must realize that God even exercises control of *the free actions of men.* We know this because the Bible says "the preparations of the heart in man and the answer of the tongue is from the Lord" (Prov. 16:1). "It is God that worketh in you," says the Apostle to the Christian, "to will and to do of his good pleasure" (Phil. 2:13). When a man determines in his own heart what he will say, or do, he may not realize that God *also* determines. But this is so. It is so even in the case of unbelievers. For "surely the wrath of man shall praise thee," says the Psalmist, "the remainder of wrath shalt thou restrain" (Ps. 76:10). This is what the Catechism means when it says that God governs "all his creatures and *all their actions.*"

There are those who want to be Christian, and yet they object to this doctrine of God's complete control of everything that happens in this world. They do want to believe that God can somehow control the world in a general way. They want to believe that God can see to it that the "over-all" picture is the way He wants it to be. But they do not want to admit that He controls the "small details." They do not want to admit that He determines the "little things" just as much as the "big things." In answer to this attitude, let us recall a well-known story. It goes like this: "For want of the general the army was defeated. For want of a horse the general was detained. For want of a shoe the horse was not available. For want of a nail the horse could have no

42

shoe." In other words, the "big" things really depend on "little" things. If the little things are not under control, the big things cannot be either. But, of course, the real difficulty that people feel when they think of God's control of everything, is this: it *seems* to reduce men to little more than "pawns on a chessboard." It *seems* to make helpless robots out of men. "If God controls everything that I do," goes the objection, "then how can I be blamed for what I do?" Or, in other words, does this doctrine not mean that people are not responsible for the things that they do? In answer to this there is only one thing we can say: we cannot understand *how* God can control everything that we do, while we are yet responsible. *We* cannot see a way to explain this truth. But it is enough for us to know that it is true. It is enough for us to know that the Bible teaches both of these things. We know from the Bible that we are responsible. We know from the Bible that we do act with real freedom (or liberty: that is, we are not being forced to act one way or the other by some power outside ourselves). And yet we also know, from the same Bible, that God does control us, so that He also determines what we do. So we accept this teaching because it is the teaching of the Bible, and not because we can explain it.

One of the strong evidences that the Bible *is* the Word of God is just exactly the fact that it teaches such doctrines as this. "The works of the Lord are *great*, sought out of all them that have pleasure therein." If we could understand everything revealed in the Bible, then this would only prove that the Bible is not the truth of God. We know that it is of God precisely because it reveals His greatness. We believe in Him and trust Him because He is able to do far more than we can even ask or think! And this, let it be observed, is vital to the faith of the Christian. If God does indeed control all things—even the very acts of wicked men (although, of course, God is not the author of sin—He controls it, but is not the author of it)—then here is the confidence of the believer: "All things work together for good to them that Love God, who are called according to his purpose" (Rom. 8:28). The Christian who believes in the God who preserves and governs all His creatures and all their actions, will not fear every crash of thunder and will not be overcome with panic in the midst of danger. He will know that his own destiny and the destiny of the whole world, are in his Father's hands. He will know that no accident can remove him before he has fulfilled the Father's plan for his life. And when sickness, trouble, or affliction does come, he will know that this too is a part of the Lord's dealings with him.

43

Questions:

1. Why is Shorty able to sleep peacefully in the midst of the storm?
2. Explain the second picture of Illustration No. 8, using Psalm 91:7 as the basis.
3. What are some of the things that God controls in this world?
4. What are some of the things that God controls that some people find hard to accept or believe?
5. Why must we hold that God controls the "little things" as much as the "big things"?
6. Does God exercise complete control over men even when they do wrong?
7. Does this make God the author of sin?
8. Can we explain this doctrine? Why?
9. Why are we to believe this doctrine?
10. Is there any comfort for the Christian in this doctrine? If so, what?
11. Read I Kings 22:1-38, and be ready to tell this story in class, as a proof of the doctrine set forth in the Catechism.

LESSON TEN

Question 12. What special act of providence did God exercise toward man in the estate wherein he was created?

Answer: When God had created man, he entered into a covenant of life with him, upon condition of perfect obedience;[1] forbidding him to eat of the tree of the knowledge of good and evil, upon the pain of death.[2]

1. But they like men [or, like Adam, ASV] have transgressed the covenant (Hos. 6:7). For Moses describeth the righteousness which is of the law, that the man which doeth those things shall live by them (Rom. 10:5).

2. But of the tree of the knowledge of good and evil, thou shalt not eat of it: for in the day that thou eatest thereof thou shalt surely die (Gen. 2:17).

From the previous Catechism question we learned that God controls all creatures and events. Here we learn how God was pleased to exercise His government of man in the beginning of human history, by means of the covenant of life (or, as it is also named, the covenant of works). As we shall see when we come to Question 20, God now exercises a special government over a portion of the human race by means of a new and better covenant, called the covenant of grace. By this covenant God brings His elect unto eternal salvation. (Compare these two covenants in Illustration 9a.) In this lesson we consider things as they were at the beginning, before man sinned against God.

According to one of the old Presbyterian Catechisms for small children, "a covenant is an agreement between two or more persons." This is true enough, when the covenant we are thinking of is between *human* persons. But this old definition is not really acceptable when we think of God's covenants with men. For in order to understand God's covenants with men, we must get rid of every thought which would suggest that God and man are equal partners therein. When God enters into a covenant with man it is not what we would call a "fifty-fifty" proposition. God does not consult with man in order to decide what the covenant will be, and what the terms of the

45

covenant will be. No, in God's covenants, His absolute sovereignty is expressed. In other words, He alone decides that there shall be a covenant. He alone decides what the terms of that covenant shall be, and He alone imposes that covenant upon himself and upon man (or men). When we keep these truths firmly in mind we will avoid the danger that might otherwise arise when we speak of the first covenant as a covenant of life or *works*. That danger—which we must always firmly resist—is that we think of man as if he could earn something from God. The Scripture clearly teaches that this is a wrong way of thinking. For even if we were to imagine a man who had never sinned—a man who had done everything that he should have done—yet even then, says Jesus, God doesn't really owe that man anything. "So likewise ye, when ye shall have done all those things which are commanded you, say, We are unprofitable servants: we have done that which was our duty to do" (Luke 17:9, 10).

Daddy, why am I an American?

In this illustration we see Shorty and his dog. In his hand he has a bone. He is going to give that bone to his dog. But before he does give it to his dog, he requires the dog to obey him by sitting at his command. Now this is not unlike a covenant given by God to man. Certainly we can see, from this illustration, that Shorty and his dog are not making any agreement. It was Shorty, and Shorty alone, who decided to give his dog this bone. And it was Shorty, and Shorty alone, who decided what "Fido" must do in order to have that bone. Neither can we say that "Fido" has really *earned* that bone. No. it would be his duty to obey Shorty even if there were no reward. If we are to speak of the "work" that "Fido" performs, then we do not mean that he has paid for his bone by this little act of obedience. It is only that Shorty has decided to make this the condition upon which he will reward his dog with the gift of that bone! So it is that when we speak of the "covenant of works," we do not mean that Adam could do anything that would make God owe him something in return. We only mean that God was pleased to require a certain obedience as the condition upon which a gift would then be given. We call the first covenant a "covenant of life," then, because it was life that God promised to Adam (as Shorty promises his dog a bone). And we also call it a "covenant of *works*," because God required

46

Adam to obey Him before He conferred the gift.

In our next two lessons we will see that Adam did not obey God, and that he brought the whole human race into an estate of sin and misery. But in the remainder of this lesson we want to point out the fact that there was nothing in the "covenant of (life, or) works" that was *unfair* to Adam or to the human race! We say this for several reasons. (1) For one thing, Adam was created with the ability that he needed in order to do what God required. "God . . . made man upright" (Eccl. 7:29). He did not have to sin. Even Satan could not *make* Adam sin. "Adam was not deceived," says the Apostle (I Tim. 2:14). He knew that Satan was tempting him to do something that he ought not to do. (2) Furthermore, God surrounded Adam with many inducements to keep him from disobedience. "Of every tree of the garden thou mayest freely eat," said the Lord (Gen. 2:16). And since all these things were "very good" (Gen. 1:31), and since God had freely offered them to Adam, there was no need to go against God's word. (3) Then, when God threatened the terrible penalty of death in case Adam should disobey, there was a very powerful reason to avoid any such disobedience. So even though it is true that we all sinned in Adam and fell with him in his first transgression, there is yet nothing unfair.

In our illustration we see Shorty and his father. "Daddy," he asks, "why am I an American?" The answer is obvious. Shorty is an American because his father and mother are Americans. The children are born with the advantages (or disadvantages) belonging to their parents. But does Shorty complain that this is "unfair"? Of course not. Rather would we suppose that he is thankful (he certainly ought to be, anyway). Likewise must we say that there was nothing unfair in the fact that we all, as members of the human race, are born in Adam's own position before God. If Adam had kept the covenant of life (or works) we too would have benefited. Now that Adam has broken that covenant we too have suffered the bitter consequences. It is nothing other than sin in our hearts, then, if we make any complaint against God because we too sinned in Adam and fell with him.

But how, it may be asked, could Satan be allowed to tempt our first parents? If God really "preserves and governs *all* His creatures and *all* their

47

actions" (Catechism Question 11), then this too must have been part of God's great plan. And if it was part of God's great plan, how can we say that it was Adam's fault alone when he sinned against God? In other words, how could God permit Satan to tempt our first parents, and how can we place the blame entirely on our first parents (*and ourselves*) that they did sin? Let us clearly understand that no one but God himself can really understand this great mystery. No human being has ever been able to explain this, and there is only one thing that we ought to do in the face of such questions. We should accept the statements of the Bible and be satisfied. The Bible simply teaches us these two things: (1) God does control all His creatures and all their actions, and (2) yet God is not the author of sin. He has kept secret just how He is able to control all without being the author of sin. We only know that this is so. He "worketh all things after the counsel of his will," says the Apostle (Eph. 1:11). And yet, "God cannot be tempted with evil, neither tempteth he any man" (James 1:13). "The Lord is righteous in all his ways, and holy in all his works" (Ps. 145:17).

In conclusion let us observe that the Catechism teaches the historical reality of Adam. In other words, the record of Genesis 1 - 3 is taken as a faithful testimony of what really happened on this earth, at a particular time and place. It is very important to stress this in our day because of the subtle danger of certain modern theologies. For more and more it has become the tendency in these theologies to deny that Adam was an actual man, and that the human race sinned in that one man and fell with him in his first transgression. These modern theologies, if they speak of Adam at all, speak as if he were only a symbol. In other words, Adam becomes a word which means, not a person by that name, but "my own tendency to sin, and fall." Suppose, in other words, that people very long ago began to realize that they were sinful, and miserable. Suppose that they then began to try to explain this fact. Then as time went by, a story was gradually developed about a garden called "paradise," and a man called "Adam." This "story" we would call a "myth." It would not be true, in the sense that it really happened. It would be "true" only in the sense that a parable may be said to be true, or a fable may be said to be true because it has a valuable moral lesson! This teaching of modern theology can be made to sound very attractive. Teachers of such error can even say that they "believe the story of Adam." But they only mean they believe in some value *in* the story. They do not mean that they believe it is a statement of what actually happened. But this we must believe. For the Bible says, "as by one man's disobedience many were made sinners, so by the obedience of one shall many be made righteous" (Rom. 5:19). To deny that Adam was a real person, as the Bible says, usually leads also to the denial that Christ is what the Bible says He is. In other words: if we do not believe what the Bible says about Adam and what he did under the covenant of life (or works), neither will we really believe what the Bible says about the Lord Jesus Christ and what He did for us in the covenant of grace!

Questions:

1. What does the word "covenant" mean?
2. How many covenants are there? Name them.
3. Is it satisfactory to say that a covenant "is an agreement between two or more people"? Why?
4. What is the chief danger to avoid in our thinking of the covenant of works?
5. How does Illustration 9 show the covenant of works?
6. What are the reasons for denying that this covenant was "unfair"?
7. How does Illustration 10 prove this?
8. What great mystery is not explained in the Bible?
9. What should we do in the face of this great mystery?
10. Would a person of modernist views say that the story of Adam is "true"? If so, what would he mean?
11. Why is it essential that we believe Genesis 1 - 3 to be history?

LESSON ELEVEN

Question 13. Did our first parents continue in the estate wherein they were created?

Answer: Our first parents, being left to the freedom of their own will, fell from the estate wherein they were created, by sinning against God.[1]

Question 14. What is sin?

Answer: Sin is any want of conformity unto, or transgression of, the law of God.[2]

Question 15. What was the sin whereby our first parents fell from the estate wherein they were created?

Answer: The sin whereby our first parents fell from the estate wherein they were created, was their eating the forbidden fruit.[3]

1. And when the woman saw that the tree was good for food, and that it was pleasant to the eyes, and a tree to be desired to make one wise, she took of the fruit thereof, and did eat; and gave also unto her husband with her and he did eat (Gen. 3:6). Lo, this only have I found, that God made man upright: but they have sought out many inventions (Eccl. 7:29).

2. Whosoever committeth sin transgresseth also the law; for sin is the transgression of the law (I John 3:4).

3. See above (Gen. 3:6).

God created man in the estate of innocence (see Appendix, Diagram A). He was God's true image, in knowledge, righteousness, and holiness. But he was not yet confirmed in that blessed condition. God set before our first parents two alternatives. On the one hand, there was the path of perfect obedience. And this path could lead only to life everlasting. "The man that doeth them [God's commandments] shall live in them," says Paul (Gal. 3:12). But, on the other hand, there was the path of disobedience. And this path could lead only to death. "For in the day that thou eatest thereof," said God

50

to Adam, speaking of the tree of the knowledge of good and evil, "thou shalt surely die" (Gen. 2:17). It is this that we are to think of when we read, in the Catechism, that our first parents were "left to the freedom of their own will." This means that our first parents had two important things.

(1) First, they had the *liberty* to follow the path of obedience unto life, or the path of disobedience unto death. We say that they had *liberty* because *there was no one forcing them* to go on either the one path or the other. Even Satan could not force them to do what he wanted them to do. He could only tempt them. He could only seek to persuade them to do what he wanted them to do, out of their own desire.

(2) Secondly, they had the *ability* to choose either one of these two alternatives. In other words, they had the power within themselves (because God had created them with the power) to do good, or evil. As we shall see, in our further studies in the Catechism, it is this power or ability to do either good or evil that was entirely lost in the fall. After the first sin, Adam and all other people descending from him remain at liberty to do either good or evil, but they do not have the power to do anything good. In this sense we must say that they lost "the freedom of their own will" which they originally had. If we say that "man has a free will," we are correct, if we mean that he is not forced to do evil by something, or someone, outside himself. But we are not correct if we mean that man, in his fallen condition, is still *able* to do good. For "there is none that doeth good, no, not one" (Rom. 3:12).

The Catechism clearly teaches that the "story" of Adam and Eve is true. This is a very important point in our day, because many false teachers deny what the Bible says. But what makes the teaching of these people so dangerous is the *way* they deny what the Bible teaches. There have always been people who have denied the teachings of the Bible, and particularly the story of the fall of man in the Garden of Eden. But what makes the present day denials so dangerous is the fact that they are not direct and plain. For example, a teacher of this sort may be willing to say, "I believe there is truth in the story of Adam and Eve. I accept it. I teach it to others." But what does he mean? Does he mean that there was one man named Adam, who lived at a particular time and place, who actually took fruit from a tree against the direct commandment of God? No, what he means is that the "story" is true very much as Aesop's Fables are "true." *True*, in the language of these modernists, does not mean that something actually happened. It only means that they see some kind of "lesson in the story." To the modernist, in other words, the story of Adam eating the forbidden fruit is nothing more

51

than a myth, or fable, that expresses (in the form of a parable) what happens in the experience of all men. To them it is not the history of what happened once. It is rather a sort of "story-picture" of what is happening all the time in everyone's experience. The reason for this false view is probably, at least for the most part, because of the teaching of evolution and other false human systems that seek to explain the existence of things without God! But we believe the story of Adam and Eve, and the fall, to be true (what really happened). Jesus accepted this account as true (see Matt. 19:4). So did the Apostle Paul (Rom. 5:12-21).

If we read again the account of the first sin (Gen. 2:17; 3:1-8), we will see one thing quite clearly. It was God alone who had the right to say "this is right," or "this is wrong." And the only way that Adam could know right and wrong safely was to remain true to God's word (Gen. 2:17). The only rule that Adam had to determine right and wrong was the command of God. That is why Satan concentrated his power of temptation upon this point. He said, "Ye shall not surely die" (Gen. 3:4). In other words, he tempted Adam to accept the thought that God's word did not have to be accepted as the only sure rule. He tempted Adam to think that he could decide for himself what was best. To express this by way of contrast, let us say that (1) God's view of sin was that "sin is any want of conformity unto or transgression of the law of God." (2) Satan's suggestion to Adam was that sin should be defined as "anything that proves to be harmful to men." These are still the only two definitions of sin. Sin is either "what is wrong because God says so," or "what is wrong because it harms us." And, of course, with the false definition of sin, we never really discover how great our sin is. Furthermore, we do not find universal agreement among men. What seems to harm one man doesn't seem to harm another. A thing that seems a sin to one man does not seem a sin to another.

But with God's definition of sin, we know exactly where we stand. The rule is the same for all men. And as you will notice in the following illustration, there are two specific kinds of sin. On the one hand (Figure A), we have sins of omission, consisting in "want of conformity unto the law. When we have a duty to perform and do not perform that duty, we lack conformity to the law of God. We are guilty because we have not done that which God requires us to do. Many people never think of this at all, when they think of sin. They think of the other kind of sin (which is the sin of commission). Because they do not swear, or steal, or murder, they imagine that they are not great sinners. And yet, they may be great sinners because

they do *not* worship God, and because they do *not* keep the Sabbath holy, etc.

On the other hand (Figure B), we see that sin can also be "transgression of the law of God." This means that we are also guilty because we do the things that God does not want us to do. The sin of Adam, in eating the forbidden fruit, was an instance of transgression.

If we keep this definition of sin in mind, we will realize that the sin of our first parents was really a terrible sin. People have sometimes said they cannot understand how such a little sin (like a boy taking an apple from the neighbor's tree) could bring such a terrible result (loss of the Garden, death, and even hell). When we see that sin is "want of conformity unto, or transgression of, the law of God"—when we see, in other words, that sin is terrible because it is against the great and good and holy *God*—we see that this is an unworthy objection. People who talk that way about sin show that they are not looking at sin in the correct way. For we must look at sin in relation to God and His law if we are to see how great it is. When we stop and think (1) that Adam went against the command of a holy God, (2) that he did so when he had full liberty and ability to do right, and (3) that he was forewarned of the terrible consequences of disobedience, then we see how great it really was.

Questions:

1. What were the two alternatives set before Adam?
2. What are the two elements of Adam's freedom of the will?
3. Which of these do *we* not have?

53

4. Do modernists believe the story of Adam to be true? Explain.
5. Why do we have to be on guard against modernist teaching about Adam?
6. State the two views of sin that Adam had to choose from.
7. What are the two kinds of (actual) sin?
8. Give an example of each.
9. Why do many people fail to realize that they are guilty sinners?
10. Why is it wrong to say that Adam's sin was a little sin?
11. State some of the reasons for maintaining that Adam's sin was a great sin.

LESSON TWELVE

Question 16. Did all mankind fall in Adam's first transgression?

Answer: The covenant being made with Adam, not only for himself, but for his posterity,[1] all mankind, descending from him, by ordinary generation, sinned in him, and fell with him, in his first transgression.[2]

Question 17. Into what estate did the fall bring mankind?

Answer: The fall brought mankind into an estate of sin and misery.[3]

1. Wherefore, as by one man sin entered into the world, and death by sin; and so death passed upon all men, for that all have sinned (Rom. 5:12).

2. By one man's disobedience many were made sinners (Rom. 5:19; see Rom. 5:12-21).

3. For all have sinned, and come short of the glory of God (Rom. 3:23). Destruction and misery are in their ways (Rom. 3:16).

In this lesson we consider one of the most difficult doctrines for human beings to accept. Just as a person who has some terrible disease like cancer hates to hear what the doctor has to say, so we, as sinners, hate to hear what the Bible says concerning our sin and misery. And yet, the strange thing is, that no one can really escape from these facts by hating to hear about them. Is it not true that all men are sinners? Is it not true that all men die (even little infants who *seem* so helpless and harmless)? If all men die and if death is the punishment for sin, how can anyone possibly deny that "all mankind" sinned in Adam "and fell with him in his first transgression"? In other words, the difference between the Christian (who accepts God's Word) and the unbeliever (who rejects God's Word) is not in the tragic fact of man's sin and misery. No, the fact of man's sin and misery is there. All *are* sinners. And all *do* die. The difference is only in the fact that the Christian has some understanding of the reason for this sin and misery. It is to this that we now direct attention.

55

(1) The first thing that we must understand is that *there is an aspect of oneness* with respect to Adam and all other members of the human race (except for Jesus Christ). There is a unity. Adam and his posterity (children) are members, one of another, in much the same way as the branches of a tree are really part of the tree. The Bible says that God "hath made *of one blood* all the nations of men for to dwell on all the face of the earth" (Acts 17:26).

Here we have an illustration of the meaning of this unity. Jesus said that an evil tree cannot bring forth good fruit. Here we see an evil tree, from which Shorty has just taken some fruit to eat. And, when he bites into that fruit, as we can see, he is very disgusted with what he finds. The fruit is rotten. And Shorty shows (and expresses) his displeasure. But why is the fruit bad? Yes, of course, it is simply because the fruit derives its entire existence from the evil tree. It is a sort of extension of it. And we would not expect anything better. For out of evil only evil can come.

In much the same way the Bible assures us that no descendant of Adam (born by ordinary generation) can possibly be other than corrupt in nature. For "who can bring a clean thing out of an unclean?" asks Job (14:4). "Or how can he be clean that is born of a woman?" (Job 25:4). It is important to observe, however, that there is one exception to this otherwise universal rule. It is for this reason that the Catechism speaks of those descending from Adam by ordinary generation, and all of those as sinning in Adam and falling with him. For our Lord Jesus Christ was not born by ordinary generation. He was not born as the natural offspring of Mary and Joseph. For it was before marriage, while Mary was yet a virgin (engaged, but not yet living with a man), that the Angel of the Lord announced to her that she would bear a son. She asked, "how shall this be, seeing I know not a man?" (Luke 1:34). "And the angel answered and said unto her, the Holy Ghost shall come upon thee, and the power of the Highest shall overshadow thee: therefore also that holy thing which shall be born of thee shall be called the Son of God (Luke 1:35). And Joseph "knew her not till she had brought forth her firstborn son" (Matt. 1:25). So Jesus was not born by ordinary

56

generation. Therefore He did not sin in Adam and fall with him. He was not born guilty or corrupt. But all other human beings, without further exception, sinned in, and fell with, Adam in his first transgression.

(2) The second thing that we must understand is that *there is also a sense in which that first sin was Adam's as it is not ours.* This is clear enough if we only ask ourselves this question: Were we actually there, as existing persons, in the Garden of Eden? Did we actually put forth our hands to take of the forbidden fruit? Well, of course, the answer is that we did not. For we were not yet in existence as individuals. When a tree is first planted there is not yet any fruit. So, when Adam was placed in the Garden we were not yet in existence. And the age-old question is: How, then, can God blame me for something that I did not actually do myself? And it is here that the illustration of the tree and its fruit fails. For in trees, and in fruit, there is no such thing as free choice. But in Adam there was. And it was because he (being left to the freedom of his own will) chose the wrong, that we are now guilty. It is this that requires further comment.

Paul says (in Rom. 5:19) that "by one man's disobedience many were made [or, constituted] sinners." In addition to the fact that Adam is the father of the human race, then, we must also say that he was the *representative head* who acted for the human race. We have already seen this in Lesson 10. And it certainly must be admitted that this seems unfair, or unjust, to many people. It seems unjust to them, because they are condemned to start with, and have no choice. It is as if they were to say: "If I only had the same chance that Adam had, I would not sin. But now God is forcing me into it whether I like it or not." The fact of the matter is, however, that God ordained our relationship with Adam before Adam sinned. The fact also is that from the first moment of our existence we are rebellious against God even as Adam himself. It is not as if God takes innocent people and places them under Adam's sin whether they like it or not. But rather it is that they are under Adam's sin as soon as they have being, and they show (by their nature, which is sinful) that they want to be sinners even as Adam. The Bible says "the wicked are estranged from the womb: they go astray as soon as they be born, speaking lies" (Ps. 58:3). In other words, they show that they approve of Adam's sin and thus are partakers of it in the fullest sense.

One of the things that has (in our opinion) created difficulties in understanding the participation of all men (except Christ) in Adam's sin is the doctrine of *creationism*. The doctrine of creationism teaches that the *body* is derived from Adam by ordinary generation, whereas the *soul* is directly

57

created by God. By this teaching the physical part of our nature comes to us from our parents, but the non-physical part (the soul, or spirit) comes to us by an act of divine creation. The body, then, on this view, is polluted or corrupted because of Adam's sin. But the soul only *becomes* sinful and polluted because it is put into a corrupt body, and because of the fact that God imputes guilt also. It does not seem that this is a biblical teaching. It seems, rather, that this teaching comes from the false Greek idea that material things (such as the body) are evil, and that the spiritual things (such as the soul) are good. It is for this reason that we believe the correct teaching to be *traducianism*. This doctrine is that the whole man (both body and soul) is received, by ordinary generation, from the parents. When the Bible says that "Adam . . . begat . . . in his own likeness, after his image," it does not refer to the body only (Gen. 5:3), but to the whole man. This view we believe to be correct for the following reasons: (a) Adam sinned in the whole man. It was not the soul alone that sinned. And it was not the body alone that sinned. It was Adam—who had both a body and a soul. (b) Scripture does not speak of God creating souls individually (as He did create the angels), and it does not speak of Him creating bodies individually. In fact, it only speaks of Him creating Adam and Eve, which He did by giving them bodies and souls. (c) If Adam had begotten only bodies, then it would not be quite possible to say that he had begotten "after his image" (Gen. 5:3), for the image does not exist in the body alone, or in the soul alone, but in the whole man. And (d) finally, the corruption of the soul is not described in the Scriptures as a result of being brought into contact (or union) with the body. It is described only as a result of participation in Adam's original sin. It was the fall that brought man into an estate of sin and misery, not the coming of the soul into contact with the body. For these reasons we believe that traducianism is to be preferred to creationism.

One of the most helpful things to consider, when we think of the fall of mankind through Adam's sin, is the parallel. In Romans 5:12-21 Paul speaks of the parallel between Adam and Christ, and between all who sinned in Adam and fell with him (on the one hand), and all who were counted righteous through the obedience of Christ (on the other hand). In this parallel there are differences as well as similarities. The main difference is that our condemnation in Adam is a matter of strict justice, while our justification in Christ is a matter of mercy only (it is a gift, in other words). But the point that we wish to emphasize here is that the very representative principle which brought death and condemnation to all men is also the means of bringing eternal life. Let us not cherish any enmity, then, against God's dealings with us in Adam. Let us acknowledge that God has done that which is right and good (even though we do not fully understand it). And let us above all make sure that we heartily embrace the offer of God's free grace in Christ, and cast ourselves upon His representative work that we might be saved. In any case: we can accomplish nothing in objecting to Adam's representation. The fact remains that we are guilty, sinful, and miserable (by nature). Explain it, or explain it not, as we may, it remains true. It is also a fact that there is no other salvation for such sinners as we are, except by the work of Jesus Christ as the representative of His people.

Questions:

1. What does "posterity" mean?
2. What does "ordinary generation" mean?
3. What facts do Christians and non-Christians have to face?
4. What is the first truth that we must understand concerning this matter?
5. How does the illustration show this? Give a scripture text in support.
6. Are all men born by "ordinary generation"? Explain.
7. What is the second truth we must understand concerning the fall?
8. What complaint does this often bring forth from sinners?
9. What false thought lies behind such complaints? State the true thought.
10. What does *creationism* teach? What does *traducianism* teach?
11. Which is to be preferred? Why? Give some reasons.
12. How does Romans 5:12-21 help us to see blessing in the representative principle?

LESSON THIRTEEN

Question 18. Wherein consists the sinfulness of that estate whereinto man fell?

Answer: The sinfulness of that state whereinto man fell consists in the guilt of Adam's first sin,[1] the want of original righteousness,[2] and the corruption of his whole nature, which is commonly called Original Sin,[3] together with all actual transgressions which proceed from it.[4]

1. By one man's disobedience many were made sinners (Rom. 5:19).

2. There is none righteous, no, not one (Rom. 3:10).

3. And God saw that the wickedness of man was great in the earth, and that every imagination of the thoughts of his heart was only evil continually (Gen. 6:5).

4. For out of the heart proceed evil thoughts, murders, adulteries, fornications, thefts, false witness, blasphemies (Matt. 15:19).

In our previous lesson we discussed original sin from the standpoint of how it is transmitted from Adam to his posterity. In this lesson we are concerned to know more about the nature of this original sin as it exists in sinful men. We will not discuss further the "guilt of Adam's first sin," as it has already been treated in our last lesson. Neither will we consider further the "want of original righteousness," which means the loss of that sinlessness that once belonged to Adam. We shall rather concentrate our attention upon the corruption of [man's] whole nature" (Consult the chart in Appendix, Diagram C.)

We often speak of the corruption of man's whole nature in these words: we say that man is *totally* depraved. And to explain what this means, let us note the following facts, as we find them expressed in Genesis 6:5 (quoted above). (1) First, we note that man's depravity (or, wickedness) is *inward*. It is deep-down within man's nature. God can see it, even if men do not. (2) Secondly, we notice that this wickedness is *great*. It is so in God's view. Men may say that they are not very wicked, but God says their wickedness is great.

(3) Thirdly, we observe that this wickedness is *continual*. It is not at some times only, but at all times, that the heart of man is wicked. (4) And finally, we see that this is *universal*. There is no one who is not evil by nature. There is not even one thought in the heart of "man" that is not wicked. Now it is to such facts as these that we refer when we speak of man's total depravity. We mean by this that sin has (like some terrible disease germ) infected every part of man's nature, and everything that man does.

But now it is very important to understand just what the *total* in total depravity means. For there are two different ways in which we can think of a thing as totally corrupt. A thing may be totally corrupt in *extent* (that is, the corruption, rottenness, or depravity may be found in every part). Or a thing may be totally corrupt in *degree* (that is, the depravity may be absolute; as bad as bad can be). And in the following illustration we see the difference between these two.

PURE   CORRUPTED IN EXTENT   CORRUPTED IN EXTENT
                                                 AND DEGREE

We first take a glass of pure water. This can be compared with Adam's original purity. Now, in the middle picture we add a drop of deadly poison, which mixes with the water and spreads out through the whole glass. The whole glass of water is now ruined. It is ruined because the poison has corrupted every part of the water. The passing of time will only allow the deadly germs to multiply and increase. So it is with man's fallen nature. But now think of a glass without anything in it except poison or disease germs. This is like the wickedness of Satan. For in him there is not even a trace of good

61

left. Wickedness has reached the fullest possible degree. And when wicked men are cast into hell, they will also be like Satan. *But* as long as they are in this world we find that evil is not yet so complete in them as it is in Satan. We say, then, that they are totally depraved in *extent* (their whole nature is corrupted by sin), but not in *degree* (evil has not gone as far as it can).

The reason why man is not yet as wicked as he can possibly become (as Satan is, and as sinners in hell are) is due to the mercy of God. Just imagine what a terrible place this world would be if all men were already as wicked as they could possibly be! Then all men would murder, and steal, and do all manner of wickedness all the time. The whole world would be filled with violence. It is doubtful that life would even continue. And observe: this is the way it would be if God did not slow down the workings of sin. How does God do this? Well, He does this in several ways. (1) For one thing, God has left in sinful men the working of a conscience. This conscience does not make a wicked man good. But it does help to restrain the workings of sin to some extent (Rom. 2:15). (2) Another thing that God has put in the world to keep sinners from doing wicked things is the power of civil government. Rulers are set in the world by God as a terror to evil men (Rom. 13:1-5). (3) Another thing that helps to hold men back from crime is the fear of death (Heb. 2:15). (4) And there is also the influence of family, education, and society which helps to retard the workings of sin in the hearts and lives of men. It is because of these things that we can even recognize a certain "good" in the lives of wicked men. From the human point of view, in other words, the wicked often act in a decent way. But we must never forget that this is not because of anything really good in them.

This brings us to focus our attention on the most important aspect of man's total depravity. It is the fact that man *cannot do anything* that God considers good, or holy, or righteous without first being regenerated by the Holy Spirit. For "the imagination of man's heart is evil from his youth" (Gen. 8:21). "The wicked are estranged from the womb: they go astray as soon as they be born, speaking lies" (Ps. 58:3). And even though sin is much restrained (as we have shown) yet the inward desire and intent of the heart is "only evil continually" (Gen. 6:5). For, as the Apostle truly says, "there is none that doeth good, no, not one" (Rom. 3:12). In other words, there is *no* person as yet not regenerated who *ever* does *anything* that pleases God. For "the Lord seeth not as man seeth; for man looketh on the outward appearance, but the Lord looketh on the heart" (I Sam. 16:7). Many people who seem good to the eye of men are not really so in the estimate of God, but are like the scribes and Pharisees of old. "Woe unto you," said Jesus, "for ye make clean the outside . . . but within . . . are full of extortion and excess . . . ye also outwardly appear righteous unto men, but within ye are full of hypocrisy and iniquity" (Matt. 23:25, 28). So certain is this, that the Bible even says that sinful men are unable to repent and turn again to God!

There are some who do not like this doctrine of man's total inability to do anything good of himself. They say that if this teaching is true, then man has no real freedom. The mistake that these people make is that they do not make a proper distinction between freedom and ability. These are not the same, although it is commonly thought that they are. Freedom is simply the absence of external (or, outward) constraint (or, force). If a person is permitted to do as he wants to do, we can surely say that he is free. But a man is not always able to do what he is free to do. Man was always free to fly. But he was not able to fly until certain devices had been invented. God is free to do anything that He wishes to do, but He is not able to lie. God cannot lie because He is controlled by His own inner nature. He is holy, and therefore He cannot lie. But that is also why man cannot do anything good (before he is regenerated by the Holy Spirit). He is *free* to do good—no one is forcing him to do evil—but he is not *able* to do good. His own inner nature, being evil, inclines him to do evil. "Can the Ethiopian change his skin, or the leopard his spots? then may ye also do good, that are accustomed to do evil" (Jer. 17:9).

We can sum it all up, then, by saying that so long as a human being is left to his own nature, he will always incline to evil more and more. This is not because he is forced that way. It is because he freely prefers it. No truth is more often taught in the Bible. Think again of how the whole human race (except for Noah and his family, who were saved by God's grace) filled the earth with violence before the flood. But even this judgment of God did not cure the tendency to evil, for we read that after the flood wicked men tried to build the tower of Babel. And then God called Abraham, and created the nation of Israel, to whom He revealed himself. But how often they too departed from God. As we read in Proverbs 1:24, "I have called, and ye refused; I have stretched out my hand, and no man regarded." Is not this the true picture of man? Does not the whole Bible lead us to this one conclusion: that man is corrupt in every part, and wholly unable to do anything good?

Questions:

1. Find a phrase in the Catechism that has the same meaning as "total depravity."
2. What facts concerning man's depravity are set forth in Genesis 6:5?
3. What is meant by *total* in "total depravity"?
4. What do we mean by speaking of the *extent* of depravity?
5. What do we mean by speaking of the *degree* of depravity?
6. Which of these properly applies to wicked men in this world? To Satan?
7. Why are wicked men not yet as wicked as they can be?
8. Do wicked men do "good things"? Explain.
9. What is meant by "total inability"?
10. Why do some disbelieve this?
11. What two things do they confuse? What does each of these mean?
12. Can God do anything evil? Why?
13. Is man free to do good? Is man able to do good? Why?
14. Prove from Bible history that unbelievers incline to more and more evil.

LESSON FOURTEEN

Question 19. What is the misery of that estate whereinto men fell?

Answer: All mankind, by their fall, lost communion with God,[1] are under His wrath and curse,[2] and so made liable to all the miseries in this life,[3] to death itself,[4] and to the pains of hell forever.[5]

1. Adam and his wife hid themselves from the presence of the Lord God (Gen. 3:8). So he drove out the man (Gen. 3:24).

2. And were by nature the children of wrath . . . (Eph. 2:3). Cursed is everyone that continueth not in all things which are written in the book of the law to do them (Gal. 3:10).

3. Wherefore doth a living man complain, a man for the punishment of his sins? (Lam. 3:29).

4. For the wages of sin is death . . . (Rom. 6:23).

5. Then shall he also say unto them on the left hand, Depart from me ye cursed, into everlasting fire, prepared for the devil and his angels (Matt. 25:41).

The human race is lost. To this everything bears witness. "For we know that the whole creation groaneth and travaileth in pain together until now" (Rom. 8:22). Unbelieving men hate to admit this. That is why they try to find some explanation of things (such as the theory of evolution) which leaves out all reference to God's wrath and curse. They try to convince themselves that the world *as it now is* can somehow be made a happy place, and that man (by his own power) can one day banish death and disease, war and strife. But this only shows how dark and vain the imagination and heart of sinful man has become. For "the wrath of God is revealed from heaven against all ungodliness and unrighteousness of men" (Rom. 1:18). And since God himself has revealed this, men must literally deceive themselves in order to avoid the truth. For the truth is that man's misery is self-evident!

As the Catechism points out, the misery of man consists (1) first of all, in the fact that *he has lost communion with God, and is under His wrath and curse.* When God created man He created him with a capacity for, and need of, eternal life. Ecclesiastes 3:11 says that God "hath set eternity in their heart" (our translation). But with the fall of man this capacity was no longer filled, and this need was no longer met. For only God could fill the heart of man. The result is that man's heart is now restless and empty. One entire book of the Bible is devoted to this subject of the vanity (emptiness) of human existence apart from God (or, "under the sun," as it is phrased, in Ecclesiastes). "Vanity of vanities, saith the preacher, vanity of vanities: all is vanity" (Eccl. 1:2). Or, as we would say today, "emptiness, emptiness, all is emptiness," or "nothingness, nothingness, all is nothingness." So in the life of those who have no saving knowledge of Christ, there is "nothing under the sun" that can fill the great void that exists in their hearts. Entertainment cannot fill that emptiness. Neither can fame, fortune, etc. The Bible says "the laughter of the fool" is like "the crackling of thorns under a pot" (Eccl. 7:6). That is, at best it (the fun and laughter) is quickly ended, with nothing left except the ashes. No doubt this is the reason why wealthy people—famous people—attractive people (such as movie personalities) often need psychiatric treatment, or become alcoholic, or even commit suicide. The more people seek to fill that place in their heart which needs the eternal God with empty things of the world, the more evident it is that the need is unsatisfied. So we can clearly see that man has indeed lost communion with God.

In the second place (2) we observe that, along with this emptiness and hopelessness, there is also *misery in this life* which none can entirely escape. As Job's friend truly said: "Man is born unto trouble as the sparks fly upward" (Job 5:7). It is only a matter of time (and the time is short at best) before disease, famine, war, or disaster will claim us all. Thus, in the Bible, man's life is described as comparable to a shadow, a dream, or a watch in the night. It is like the flower, or the grass, that hardly comes to full growth before it begins to fade quickly away. Not all have the same experience, of course. A dread disease will smite one. Another will fall in battle. We may even see a godly man (like Job) suffering, while a wicked man (for the moment) is "not in trouble" (Ps. 73:5). We cannot explain these "differences," other than to say that they are all a part of the wise and sovereign plan of God. His momentary blessings for the wicked only make their doom more terrible. And His momentary chastisements and trials for the righteous only work out for good in the end. But the important point is that misery is the universal and inescapable portion of all men. There are

66

pains of body, and sorrows of soul, that no man can be a complete stranger to in this life.

In the third place (3) there is *the universal dominion of death.* In this also all men have their portion. For "it is appointed unto men once to die" (Heb. 9:27). It is true, of course, that the glory of the Christian faith is that it promises victory over death. But for the present, death is an enemy yet to be destroyed (I Cor. 15:26). It was because of this that our Lord himself, when He came to the tomb of Lazarus, wept, and "groaned in the spirit" being "troubled" (John 11:34, 35). It is not according to Scripture to make light of death, or to treat it (as modernists often do) as a natural thing (like birth). No, death too is caused by sin, and is a part of man's misery.

And finally (4) we notice that there is *the everlasting punishment* of the lost. Since this is a subject of which we will learn more later (Q. 28, 84), we will here present only a brief discusssion. But let us emphasize that this solemn truth was taught in a particularly full and clear manner by our Lord Jesus Christ. It was He (more than any prophet or apostle) who warned us of this. He speaks of "unquenchable fire" (Matt. 3:12), the "worm that dieth not and the fire that is not quenched" (Mark 9:48), the "torment in fire and brimstone" (Rev. 14:10), "the outer darkness" and the "weeping and gnashing of teeth" (Matt. 8:12). And it was our Lord who used the same word to describe the everlasting punishment of the lost, and the everlasting blessedness of the saved! (see Matt: 25:46).

It is important to understand that *all mankind* was brought by Adam's dis-

obedience into an estate of misery. But it is also important to understand that those who belong to the Lord Jesus Christ are really in a different position from those who are unbelieving. (1) Let us first consider the differences that pertain to this present life. Here we must understand that the believer once again enjoys communion with God. He can come to God through Jesus Christ. And God comes to that believer through the Holy Spirit. Furthermore, by the sacrifice of Jesus Christ the wrath and curse of God is taken away from that believer. He no longer fears that God will punish him forever, since Christ has been punished for him. He is no longer overwhelmed by the fear of death, and of everlasting punishment. Now observe that in none of these things is the believer completely delivered, as yet, from the estate of misery He does not yet have full and perfect communion with God (he is weak and sinful yet, and beset by many difficulties). And there is yet a sense in which the believer too is punished by God. "For whom the Lord loveth he chasteneth, and scourgeth every son whom he receiveth" (Heb. 2:6). So in the life of the believer too there comes sickness, sorrow, etc. But the difference is that it no longer comes as an expression of the wrath and curse of God, but as a corrective discipline.

(2) It is at death that the difference between the believer and the unbeliever becomes yet more pronounced. For then it is that the believer discovers the full blessedness of the fact that when he was brought to Christ (during his lifetime) his soul was already brought from death unto life. Now, at death, he discovers that death has no sting for him (because the soul has already passed out of the power of death). He discovers that nothing can separate him from Christ. The body alone dies and it only dies "for a while," that is, until the last day when it shall be raised again from the grave. Whereas, in the case of the unbeliever, it is both body and soul that experience "the death" of separation from God and inexpressible suffering. The soul of the unbeliever is already dead (Eph. 2:1). It has *not* passed from death unto life. Now God's wrath—which remains upon him— is suddenly felt in greater measure.

(3) But it is not until the last day—when there is to be a general resurrection of all men—that we finally see the believer completely delivered from *all* misery whatsoever, and brought to a complete happiness. And it is only then, too, that we see the unbeliever delivered over unto complete misery in both body and soul which will never end. "Be not afraid of them that kill the body," said Jesus, "and after that have no more that they can do. But I will forewarn you whom ye shall fear: fear him, which after he hath killed hath

power to cast into hell; yea, I say unto you, fear him" (Luke 12:4, 5). "Fear him which is able to destroy both soul and body in hell" (Matt. 10:28).

Questions:

1. What is the great truth that unbelievers hate to admit?
2. What do they attempt to do because of this hatred?
3. What are the four parts of the misery of man?
4. How can we see that man has lost communion with God?
5. How can we see that man is under God's wrath and curse?
6. What are some of the miseries of this life?
7. What book of the Bible vividly describes man's loss of communion with God?
8. What does this book of the Bible mean by "vanity"?
9. What are some of the ways in which people try to make up for this loss?
10. Do all men experience the same miseries? Explain.
11. What do the illustrations teach concerning the misery of man?
12. Do believers as well as unbelievers experience misery?
13. What is the difference between the experience of believers and unbelievers in this life? At death? In the world to come?
14. How do we know there is really a hell?
15. If all men must die, what does the Bible mean by saying that the believer has already passed from death unto life?
16. Does God have a good purpose in the miseries that yet must be experienced by true believers? Explain.

LESSON FIFTEEN

Question 20. Did God leave all mankind to perish in the estate of sin and misery?

Answer: God having, out of His mere good pleasure, from all eternity, elected some to everlasting life,[1] did enter into a covenant of grace, to deliver them out of the estate of sin and misery, and to bring them into an estate of salvation by a Redeemer.[2]

1. According as he hath chosen us in him, before the foundation of the world (Eph. 1:4).

2. But now the righteousness of God without the law is manifested, being witnessed by the law and the prophets: even the righteousness of God which is by faith of Jesus Christ unto all and upon all them that believe (Rom. 3:21, 22).

We have thus far traced the history of man from the state of innocency (see Appendix, Diagram A), in which he was created, to the state of sin and misery, into which he fell. With this question of the Catechism we begin to see unfolded before us the wonderful account of God's mercy to sinners. Here we see *how* He brings them out of the estate of sin and misery, and into the estate of salvation.

It is of God's mercy or grace *alone* that there is a way of escape for sinful men. It is also by God's power *alone* that sinful men are enabled to make escape from the estate of sin and misery. Thus we come to what Reformed Christians usually call the doctrine of God's *unconditional* (or unmerited) *election.* This doctrine teaches: (1) that God has chosen, out of the total number of lost men, a certain portion (or, number) to be saved; (2) that God does not choose these persons because of anything good in them. God's election is unconditional because He does not find some condition in the elect that He does not find in the non-elect; (3) that God has chosen these people to be saved through Jesus Christ alone. They cannot be saved, in other words, except by being—in due time—brought to Christ, justified, adopted, etc.; (4) and that this unconditional election was made from all eternity. In other words, it always was God's purpose to save these persons—even before they were born, yes, even before the world itself was created.

We cannot illustrate all of these points. But we can see the principal emphasis in the following illustration:

All toys are equal. One is no better than the other. None deserves to be chosen by Shorty more than the others! Why then does Shorty say, "I'll take *this* one"? The reason cannot be found in the toys, since there is no difference between them. The condition of one was just the same as the condition of the other! The reason for choosing "this one" rather than "that one," then, must be found entirely in Shorty. This illustrates what we mean when we say that God's election is unconditional. We simply mean that the reason for God's choosing this man, and not that man, is not in them, but in God only.

There is no doctrine that has been more hated by sinful men. And yet, neither is there any doctrine more clearly taught in Scripture. The Bible says that God "hath chosen us in him before the foundation of the world . . . having predestinated us unto the adoption of children . . ." (Eph. 1:4, 5). The very word *predestinate* simply means "to determine beforehand the destiny of a person." "Ye have not chosen me," said Jesus to His disciples, "but I have chosen you" (John 5:16). Anyone with even the least knowledge of the Bible will certainly realize the importance of this truth! "Your fathers dwelt on the other side of the flood in old time," said Joshua to the Israelites, "even Terah, the father of Abraham, and the father of Nachor: *and they served other gods. And I took your Father Abraham . . .*" (Josh. 24: 2, 3). "The Lord thy God hath chosen thee to be a special people unto himself," said Moses, "above all the people that are upon the face of the earth" (Deut. 7:6). Even when we come to what the Scripture says about those who were, and were not, true believers within the nation of Israel, it is the same. "Israel hath not obtained that which he seeketh for but the election hath obtained it, and the rest were blinded" (Rom. 11:7). "Even so," says Paul, speaking of himself and others who had believed in the Lord Jesus Christ, while many Jews had rejected Him, "then at this present time also there is a remnant according to the election of grace" (Rom. 11:5).

The question that always arises in our minds as we think about this

71

doctrine of unconditional election is this: _why_ has God chosen "this man" and not "that man"? Or in other words it seems to sinful men as if this were not quite fair! But the truth is that all men deserve damnation. And if all men deserve damnation, it cannot possibly be "unfair" if they get what they deserve! God does no wrong to any when He gives some men the punishment they deserve, while giving others the mercy they do not deserve. "Is it not lawful for me to do what I will with mine own? Is thine eye evil, because I am good?" says Jesus (Matt. 20:15). It is wicked to complain against God when He gives some men what they deserve. Another question that arises is this: the doctrine of unconditional election seems to make salvation completely "automatic." In other words, as some say, "If God has chosen me to be saved, then I will be saved no matter what I do." This is a common reaction among sinners. But it is entirely wrong. For when people think of election in this way, they do not think correctly. The Bible does _not_ teach that men will be saved "automatically." It does not teach that men will be saved "no matter what they do." The Bible teaches that God has "chosen us in him," that is, in Christ. God has chosen men for a certain destiny, yes, but He has also chosen them for a certain relationship which leads to that end. As Paul says, "whom he did predestinate, them he also called: and whom he called, them he also justified: and whom he justified, them he also glorified" (Rom. 8:29). In our Catechism studies we will presently go on to see how God's elect are brought, step by step, to their appointed destiny. But here we simply need to see the fact that this idea of being saved "no matter what we do" is a false idea. If a man is elect it does matter what he does. For he must repent of his sins, believe on the Lord Jesus Christ, and be saved according to His plan.

It is for this reason that the Catechism speaks of the elect as being saved _in_ the "covenant of grace." In Lesson 10 we considered the "covenant of life," or (as it is also designated) "the covenant of works." Here we saw quite clearly that no man was "automatically" lost. No man was brought to an estate of sin and misery for no reason, and without any regard to anything else. Rather do we see that all men who are brought into the estate of sin and misery are brought into that estate because they were created in union with Adam, and because they sinned in Adam and fell with him in his first transgression. So it is with the second covenant. For just as God originally dealt with all men through Adam, the representative head of the whole human race, in the covenant of life; so God now deals with His elect people through Jesus Christ, the representative head of the new race of God's people, in the covenant of grace. Looking at the matter this way: (1) the parties in the covenant of grace are the Father and the Son (as a representative person); (2) the condition of this covenant is that Christ (by partaking of human nature) fulfill all the demands of the law in order to receive the promise of life to give to His people; and (3) the promise of the Father is to grant eternal life to all those represented by Jesus Christ. It is only in union with Christ, therefore, that any benefits are given to sinful men. And this means that no one can possibly receive any benefits unless he repents, believes, etc. (except, of course, in the case of infants or insane persons).

Another reaction is commonly observed. People say, "If I am not elected then there is nothing that I can do about it, no matter how much I might want to be saved." The thought here is that a man could want to be saved and that God would not want him saved, or that a man could be willing to come to Christ but that He would not be willing to receive him if he did come. This does seem logical to the human mind, darkened by sin as it is. But we can be sure from the teaching of the Bible that things are not what they seem to man's sinful mind. As a matter of fact the Bible clearly teaches that (a) no man wants to be saved in the way that God requires, unless and until God gives a new heart. "Thy people shall be willing," says the Psalmist, "in the day of thy power!" (Ps. 110:3). (b) The Bible also teaches that no man who wants to be saved in God's way—who is willing to come to Christ, in other words—will be lost. And (c) the Bible also teaches that those who do not want to be saved by coming to Christ in repentance and faith are wholly to blame for this fact. They cannot say they are unwilling to come because God did not elect them. No, the unwillingness is entirely due to their own sinful preference for not coming to Him.

The doctrine of unconditional election is awe-inspiring. It is mysterious (we cannot fully understand all that is involved). But the important thing to realize is that this is what the Bible teaches; God has chosen some men, and not others. And He has done this without any injustice. He has done this so that there will be two, and only two results. On the one hand there will be some who are saved. And when they at last reach heaven they will say this: "I owe it all to God. I did not deserve this. But God chose me, and to Him alone be the praise." But, on the other hand, there will be others who are lost. And when they at last reach their sad destination they will only be able to say this: "It is all my own fault. I deserve this. I deserved it because I sinned in Adam and fell with him. But I also deserve it even more because I did not want to come to Christ in true repentance and faith. I did not

73

choose Christ, and to me alone be the blame." It is only when we see these two things: on the one hand, no ground to boast (not even one little thing of self); and on the other hand, no ground to complain: that we can begin to understand the importance and wonder of this doctrine. And, as far as any personal difficulties are concerned, let us always put this truth first—if we really want to be saved in God's way then we need not fear—"give diligence to make your calling and election sure," says Peter, "for if ye do these things, ye shall never fall: for so an entrance shall be ministered unto you abundantly into the everlasting kingdom of our Lord and Saviour Jesus Christ" (II Peter 1:10).

Questions:

1. Give a clear statement of what is meant by "unconditional election."
2. *Why* has God chosen the persons He has chosen?
3. *When* has God chosen them?
4. What are the truths concerning this doctrine shown in the illustration?
5. Is this doctrine plainly taught in Scripture? If so, where? Give an example.
6. Is unconditional election unfair to those who are not elected? Why?
7. Does election make salvation "automatically certain" for the elect? Why?
8. How are the elect saved?
9. What are some of the things that the elect will certainly do?
10. Why must the elect come to Christ?
11. Can all who want to be saved be saved? Explain.
12. What two great truths does this doctrine help us to see?

LESSON SIXTEEN

Question 21. Who is the Redeemer of God's elect?

Answer: The only Redeemer of God's elect is the Lord Jesus Christ,[1] who, being the eternal Son of God, became man,[2] and so continueth to be, God and man in two distinct natures, and one person,[3] for ever.[4]

1. For there is one God, and one mediator between God and men, the man Christ Jesus (I Tim. 2:5).

2. And the Word was made flesh, and dwelt among us (John 1:14).

3. Whose are the fathers, and of whom as concerning the flesh Christ came, who is over all, God blessed for ever. Amen (Rom. 9:5).

4. But this man, because he continueth ever, hath an unchangeable priesthood (Heb. 7:24).

The Scripture can be understood only by those who are careful to note the small word *only*. For this word is used to teach us some of the most important things that we must know in order to be saved. "Thou shalt worship the Lord thy God," said Jesus, "and him *only* shalt thou serve" (Matt. 4:10). Scripture speaks of "the *only* true God" (John 17:3), and of Jesus as the "*only* begotten Son" (John 3:16). And how important the word *only* is in each of these texts! It is also very important in the Catechism statement. For Jesus Christ is the only Redeemer of the elect. "Neither is there salvation in any other: for there is none other name under heaven given among men, whereby we must be saved" (Acts 4:12). God alone is to be worshiped and served. But Jesus said, "no man cometh unto the Father, but by me" (John 14:6). We see, then, that "whosoever denieth the Son, the same hath not the Father" (I John 2:23). And never was this teaching more important than it is today. This is because the modern ecumenical movement has fostered *the universalist view* of salvation. This is the conception which says that there is saving truth in all religions for those who are sincere and earnest. It is for this reason that there has been a great change in the conception of Christian missions among churches belonging to the World Council of Churches. Instead of sending out missionaries to preach the gospel of Jesus Christ as the only hope for lost sinners, they now send forth people who are willing to listen as well as speak—to learn as well as teach—and thus by what is called "dialogue" (two-way conversation) the end result may be a new religion altogether. This new religion will supposedly incorporate all that is "good" from the various religions (including Christianity). Now against this view, we must take our stand. We must steadfastly maintain that Jesus Christ is the *only* Redeemer of God's elect. For no matter what men say, there is only one way (the narrow way) which leads to life. And all who do not receive Him as He is offered in the gospel are on the broad road that leads to destruction.

But why is Jesus the only Redeemer of God's elect? The answer is that Jesus *alone* is qualified to be our Redeemer because of His eternal deity and true humanity. Let us think for a moment of what this means. (1) It means that Jesus Christ *is* God. He is of one substance (or essence) with the Father and the Holy Spirit. In other words, He is infinite, eternal, and unchangeable, in His being, wisdom, power, holiness, justice, goodness, and truth. There is no way in which we should honor the Father that we should not also honor the Son. We know this from four things that we find in Scripture. (a) Jesus Christ is *called* God (Isa. 9:6; John 20:28). (b) He has the *attributes* of God (John 1:1; 2:24, 25). (c) He is able to do the mighty *works* of God (John 5:21; Col. 1:16). (d) And He is given the *worship* that belongs properly to God (John 20:28; Rev. 5:12-14). From such biblical evidence as this, we see that there are many today who really deny the Christ of the Bible. There are those, for example, who believe that Jesus only *became* divine (Jehovah's Witnesses). They say that God the Father created Jesus, and that He is only "a god" in comparison with the Father. Many modernists also believe that Jesus became divine, but not that He is God as truly as the Father and the Holy Spirit. And sometimes evangelical Christians *act as if* they did not believe Jesus to be God in the same high sense as the Father and the Spirit. This is seen from the fact that they make (or make use of) pictures of Jesus. Strange that people should think it idolatrous to make any graven image or likeness of the Father, or the Spirit, while thinking nothing of it when it comes to the Son. Yet all the while Jesus is equal with the Father and the Spirit in power and glory, and is of the same substance with them!

Now this divine person (who always was God, in the full sense), in the moment of time appointed, became man by taking to himself a complete

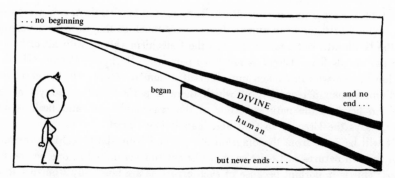

... no beginning

began

DIVINE

human

and no
end . . .

but never ends . . . .

human nature. Or, as John expresses it, "the Word *became* flesh and dwelt among us" (John 1:14). Let us try to illustrate this mystery:

Since we will discuss in our next section the *way* in which the Word became flesh, we here focus attention upon the result of this event. The result was that God the Son became man without ceasing to be God. Or, to express the same truth in different words, the divine nature was united to the human nature without "conversion, composition, or confusion." (1) There were some in the ancient Church, for example, who felt that the incarnation (Christ's taking unto himself a human nature) would of necessity result in a change of either one or the other of these two natures. Some believed that the divine nature would be reduced (by His becoming man) so that He would no longer be the same in substance, and equal with the Father and the Spirit. Others thought that His human nature would be lifted up so greatly by being united to His divine nature, that He would no longer be "one of us" in all things except sin. Against this, the Catechism maintains that His divine nature remained truly and completely divine, and the human likewise human. (2) Others believed that the incarnation must have brought a mixture of the two natures, so that Jesus would have neither divine nor human nature, but rather a new nature midway between these two. This would be similar to taking two parts of hydrogen and one part of oxygen (two different gases) in order to make water (which is not a gas, but a liquid). (This view is similar to the doctrine of Jehovah's Witnesses. They do not view our Lord as truly God, nor as truly man, but as something "in between.") Against this view also the Catechism maintains the integrity of both natures in Christ. (3) Some were ready to agree with the orthodox view that Jesus had two natures which were neither changed nor mixed, but they made the mistake of thinking that in order for this to be true He must have had two

77

different (or separate) personalities. They saw in Christ, then, two persons—the divine Christ, and the human Jesus—very much as they saw three persons in the Godhead. But against this too the Catechism (along with all orthodox creeds) stands firm. Christ is not "two persons." He is one Person. He is a divine Person who has taken unto himself a human nature. He therefore has a divine-human personality, in which there is perfect unity, and yet a distinction between the natures. "For as the reasonable soul and flesh is one man," says the Creed, "so God and man is one Christ."

It will be seen, from the diagram above (and from the Catechism answer) that the two natures of Christ remain distinct and yet united in one person for ever. This is important because of such errors as are taught by Roman Catholics and Lutherans. Both of these denominations teach that the human nature of Christ is *now* able to be present in many different places at the same time. (They say that the human nature of Christ is now *ubiquitous*.) Against this we see the clear statements of the Bible. "He is not here, but is risen" (Luke 25:6). And Him "the heaven must receive until the times of restitution of all things" (Acts 3:21). Even the Lord's Supper is "in remembrance of" Christ, rather than the physical presence. What the Catechism properly insists upon, then, is that Christ is also at this very moment just as truly possessed of two natures—the divine and the human—as when He was on this earth. His human nature (a true body and a reasonable soul) is located in one place now, as truly as it was then.

In summing up the simple, and yet profound, truth of this lesson, we mention the fact that it is contained in the phrase "the Lord Jesus Christ." (1) The word "Lord" is really the same as Jehovah. It traces back to the great "I am that I am," the declaration of the self-existent and self-sufficient God. *This* Jesus Christ is. (2) The word "Jesus" is the same as the biblical Joshua. And while the name has rich significance in other ways too, it certainly is a name that indicates the reality of our Lord's human nature. (3) The word "Christ" means "the anointed one." It indicates the fact that He is the Messiah. And here, in these three words, we have the essence of what the Catechism is teaching us: "the only Redeemer . . . being the eternal Son of God (Lord), became man (Jesus), and so was, and continueth to be, God and man in two distinct natures (Lord and Jesus), and one person (Christ), for ever."

Questions:

1. Why is the word "only" so important in this Catechism question?

78

2. What do "universalists" teach? What movement teaches universalism?
3. What is "dialogue"? What is the purpose of it?
4. Why is Jesus the only Redeemer?
5. How do we know that Jesus Christ is *God*?
6. Give examples of denials of the deity of Christ.
7. Is it wrong to make (or use) pictures of Christ? Why?
8. In the diagram what does the endless beam represent? What does the other beam represent?
9. What are some of the ways in which the teaching set forth in the Catechism (and diagram) have been denied? Give three.
10. What is the false teaching of Roman Catholicism and Lutheranism? Explain.
11. Show that this is false from Scripture.
12. How does this phrase, "the Lord Jesus Christ," sum up the teaching of this lesson? Explain.

LESSON SEVENTEEN

Question 22. How did Christ, being the Son of God, become man?

Answer: Christ, the Son of God, became man by taking to himself a true body,[1] and a reasonable soul,[2] being conceived by the power of the Holy Ghost, in the womb of the Virgin Mary, and born of her,[3] yet without sin.[4]

1. Forasmuch then as the children are partakers of flesh and blood, he also himself likewise took part of the same (Heb. 2:14).
2. Then saith he unto them, my soul is exceeding sorrowful, even unto death (Matt. 26:38).
3. Behold, thou shalt conceive in thy womb and bring forth a son, and shalt call his name Jesus (Luke 1:31). The Holy Ghost shall come upon thee, and the power of the Highest shall over shadow thee (Luke 1:35).
4. Such an high priest became us, who is holy, harmless, undefiled, separate from sinners (Heb. 7:26).

In the previous lesson we learned that Christ, being the eternal Son of God, became man. We learned that He also continues to be God and man, in two distinct natures, the one person, forever. In this lesson we go on to ask *how* this came to be so. And in order to open the discussion of this subject, we begin by comparing the Roman Catholic and the Reformed conception of the virgin birth of Christ.

In the Roman Catholic conception the emphasis falls upon the word *virgin!* It is Mary who receives the attention. And the result is that she is lifted up. She is hailed as the Mother of God, and as the Queen of heaven. In the Reformed conception it is Christ who receives the attention. And the emphasis falls upon the word *birth!* Even though Christ was the eternal Son of God, yet was He born (in the fullness of time) the son of man. This means that He was humbled. This means that He was brought low. He who was far above mere human creatures (as the Creator and God of all) lowered himself to their level. And He even wore the crown of thorns, in suffering the damnation of sinners in the place of many.

In order to avoid misunderstanding of this important teaching of the Bible and the Catechism, we must ask the question: Is it proper to speak of Mary as the Mother of God? As can be seen from the diagram above, this phrase, "Mary the Mother of God," is often used to exalt Mary. When this phrase is used to lift Mary up to the level of God, then it is utterly false, and against the honor of God. But, at the same time, it is important to understand that this same phrase can be used to mean something very true and very proper. The Bible, and the Catechism, teach us that Jesus Christ is a person. They also teach us that this Person has two natures. He is God and He is man. And this means that Jesus was God (as well as man) when He was born of Mary. The child that Mary brought forth was the God-man. And therefore Mary is the mother of Jesus, who is God. In this sense it is not only proper, but even quite necessary to say that Mary is the Mother of God. But observe that this is said not to lift Mary up to the level with God. It is said only because Jesus truly did come down to the same level with Mary.

Two errors must be avoided if we are to have a true conception of this wonderful event spoken of in this Catechism question. (1) And the first error is that which confuses virginity with sinlessness. When the Roman Catholic Church speaks of the Virgin Mary, it does not mean that Mary was merely a virgin up until the time when Jesus was born. No, according to the Roman Catholic teaching, Mary always remained a virgin even after that. In other words, according to the Roman Catholic Church, Mary never had sexual relations with her own husband. Let it be said quite plainly that this is a very wicked teaching. If Mary had married Joseph (which she did) and then

81

refused to have sexual relations with him, she would have been guilty of a sin against her husband and her God (see I Cor. 7:3-5). The Bible says that Joseph "knew her not *till* she had brought forth her *firstborn* son" (Matt. 1:25). This clearly shows that he *did* know her after Jesus was born. Now the reason for this teaching of the Roman Catholic Church is this: it is the idea that virginity in Mary was necessary in order for Mary to be holy, and that Mary had to be holy in order for Jesus to be born without sin. (2) The second error is that of the modernists, who are not willing to accept anything miraculous. Many of them hold that Christ was not even sinless. But even those modernists who may be willing to say He was sinless will insist that He need not have been virgin born to be sinless. They say that even if He were the natural son of both Mary and Joseph, He still could have been sinless, and still God incarnate in human nature. But Jesus said "that which is born of the flesh is flesh" (John 3:6). In other words, if Jesus were born as others are (by ordinary generation—of a human mother and father) He would indeed have a sinful nature. This does not mean that sexual relations between husband and wife are sinful. But it does mean that children born as a result of this sexual relationship are born sinful. (It is not the *process* that is wrong, but the *product* which is sinful.)

The true doctrine, in other words, is that the virgin birth was necessary because only through a miracle could Jesus Christ be born with a true human nature and yet without sin. And this was because of the power of the Holy Spirit, and not any holiness or virtue belonging to the virgin Mary herself. "The Holy Ghost shall come upon thee," said the angel to Mary, "and the power of the Highest shall overshadow thee: therefore also that holy thing which shall be born of thee shall be called the Son of God" (Luke 1:35). To say that Mary was "overshadowed" is the same as to say that in spite of her being a sinful human being (as all human beings except Christ are), the Holy Ghost would see to it that her child was not sinful. And when we read that "therefore" this holy one would be born of her, we clearly see that it was not what Mary was, but rather what the Holy Ghost did, that explains the basis of this miracle. And so, as the Catechism says, Christ *took* a human nature from Mary, and did it in such a way that her own sinfulness was not taken with it.

When the Catechism speaks of a "true body," it means that Jesus took unto himself the same kind of body that we ourselves possess (except for sin). This point is stressed because of a heresy known as "Docetism." In early Christian history there were some who held that Christ only *seemed* (or appeared) to have a physical body. They said that God could not really have a human body, that He could not really suffer and die. This teaching is not common today. Much more common today is the denial of the deity of Christ. But there are some, such as the Coptic Church in parts of Africa, who still believe in the deity of Christ (that He was God) while not believing in His humanity (that He had a true body and a reasonable soul). When the Catechism says that Jesus had a "reasonable soul," it means that just as we have a body and a soul, so Christ also had a human soul as well as a human body. In the early history of the Church there were those who admitted that Jesus had a "true body," but did not admit that He also had "a reasonable soul." They thought that the divine nature (Christ as God) took the place of a soul within His body. But this too is a denial of that which Scripture clearly teaches, and of that which is necessary to our salvation. Just as the Bible speaks of Christ's hunger, thirst, pain, etc. (which prove that He had a true body), so it also speaks of His feeling sorrow and grief, and of His increasing in wisdom, etc. (which prove that He also had a reasonable soul). As the Bible says, "in *all* things it behoved him to be made like unto his brethren, that he might be a merciful and faithful high priest in things pertaining to God, to make reconciliation for the sins of the people. For in that he himself hath suffered being tempted, he is able to succour them that are tempted" (Heb. 2:17, 18).

It is important to emphasize the fact that without this doctrine of the virgin birth of Christ there is no gospel of salvation for sinners. This is clearly brought out in two questions that we find in the Westminster Larger Catechism. "Why was it requisite that the Mediator should be God?" "It was requisite that the Mediator should be God, that He might sustain and keep the human nature from sinking under the infinite wrath of God, and the power of death; give worth and efficacy to His sufferings, obedience and intercession; and to satisfy God's justice, procure His favor, purchase a peculiar people, give His Spirit to them, conquer all their enemies, and bring them to everlasting salvation." In other words, there was a great work to be done—a work so great that none could possibly do it but one who is very God. But at the same time, we ask, "Why was it requisite that the Mediator should be man?" "It was requisite that the Mediator should be man, that He might advance our nature, perform obedience to the law, suffer and make intercession for us in our nature, have a fellow-feeling of our infirmities; that we might receive the adoption of sons, and have comfort and access with boldness unto the throne of grace." Since it was man who

83

needed saving, in other words, and this could be done only by the obedience of man, it was also necessary that Christ be truly human. And "it was requisite that the Mediator, who was to reconcile God and man, should himself be both God and man, and this in one person, that the proper works of each nature might be accepted of God for us, and relied on by us, as the works of the whole person." Or in other words, the Savior that I must have is the Savior who is able to reach me—and to reach God—and this Christ alone can do. He can do this because He is God and man, in two distinct natures, and one Person, forever.

Questions:

1. In the diagram what are some of the false points of the Roman Catholic teaching that are brought out?
2. What are some of the correct points in the Reformed teaching here shown?
3. Is it proper to speak of Mary as "the Mother of God"? Explain.
4. What does the Roman Catholic Church confuse virginity with?
5. Was Mary a virgin after Jesus was born? Prove.
6. What is the error of the modernists with respect to Christ's birth?
7. Why was it necessary for Christ to be born of a virgin?
8. Why did the Holy Ghost overshadow Mary? (Luke 1:35).
9. What is meant by "true body"? What heresy denied that Christ had this?
10. What is meant by "reasonable soul"? How did early heretics deny this?
11. Prove that Jesus had both a true body and a reasonable soul.
12. Is this doctrine essential for our salvation? Give some reasons.

LESSON EIGHTEEN

Question 23. What offices doth Christ execute as our Redeemer?

Answer: Christ, as our Redeemer, executeth the offices of a prophet,[1] of
a priest,[2] and of a king,[3] both in his estate of humiliation and
exaltation.

1. Moses truly said unto the fathers, A prophet shall the Lord your God raise
up unto you of your brethren, like unto me: him shall ye hear in all
things whatsoever he shall say unto you (Acts 3:22).

2. Thou art a priest for ever, after the order of Melchisedec (Heb. 5:6).

3. Yet have I set my king upon my holy hill of Zion (Ps. 2:6).

In order to bring out the importance of this part of the Catechism, we will
begin by showing the relationship between various aspects of our Christian
faith. For the truth expressed in this Catechism answer touches upon (1)
man's original constitution, (2) the Old Testament history of the preparation
for man's redemption, (3) the saving work of Christ, (4) the conversion of
sinners, and (5) the marks of a true Church. We represent these in the
following chart:

	PROPHET	PRIEST	KING
Man As he was (See also Lesson 8) As he is	KNOWLEDGE - - - - - - - - - - ignorance	RIGHTEOUSNESS - - - - - - - - - - guilt	HOLINESS - - - - - - - - - - sinfulness
Israel	MOSES and the PROPHETS	AARON and his HOUSE	DAVID and his HOUSE
Christ	THE WORD OF GOD ("revealing to us")	THE SACRIFICE ("offering up himself")	KING OF KINGS ("subduing us, etc.")
Conversion	KNOWLEDGE (law and gospel)	FEELING (my need of Christ)	WILL (accept free offer)
A true CHURCH	FAITHFUL PREACHING OF THE WORD OF GOD	RIGHT ADMINISTRATION OF THE SACRAMENTS	PROPER EXERCISE OF DISCIPLINE

When God created man, He created him after His own image (Q. 10). Man originally had true knowledge, righteousness, and holiness. Thus we can say that he was virtually (that is, in effect) a prophet, priest, and king (see Lesson 10). When Adam sinned and fell, we sinned and fell with him. And so all men (except for Jesus Christ) became ignorant, guilty, and sinful. And the whole message of the Bible is about what God has done to save some men from this lost condition.

The Old Testament tells us what God did to prepare for the day when He would send forth His Son to save His people. And one of the things we notice throughout the Old Testament history is that it centers around those men who were chosen by God to serve as prophets, priests, and kings. At first these offices were not so clearly distinguished. Abraham was a prophet (Gen. 20:7). But he also offered up sacrifices (Gen. 13:4). And he also seems to have been a king (Gen. 14:1, 2, 13, 17-24). But as soon as Abraham's family grew large enough to be a nation, God appointed that different men would hold these offices alongside one another. God appointed Moses as a prophet in a special sense, and promised that other prophets would follow him until "the last great prophet" came (Deut. 18:15-20). He also appointed Aaron as the High Priest of Israel, commanding that his sons should follow after him in this office (Ex. 29:29). Later it was revealed that the succession of priests too would finally end when Christ came (I Sam. 3:35ff.). And then, when David was appointed King in Israel, God also promised that his house (or, line) would continue until a Son was born who would sit upon the throne forever (II Sam. 7:12-16; Ps. 2; 72; 110, etc.). There were, of course, unfaithful men in these offices as well as faithful men. Through faithful prophets God gave His true word. Through faithful priests God showed how there could be no forgiveness of sin without the shedding of blood. Through faithful kings God showed how His people were to obey Him in all things. And through the unfaithful—prophets, priests, and kings— (and even the best were not always faithful) God made men realize that salvation would never be fully and perfectly accomplished until the promised Messiah came. This became especially clear when, toward the close of the Old Testament period, evil days came upon Israel.

When Jesus Christ at last came, He not only completed (or, fulfilled) each of these three offices, but He also united them in one great work of redemption. (1) We see this, first of all, during His career here on earth. (a) He spoke as no man ever spoke before, or since. He himself was the truth. He was God's full revelation of himself. In Him (and in the record of what

He did) God's Word is complete. (b) He made the one final and sufficient sacrifice for the sins of many. He did this by offering himself as a sacrifice on the cross. (c) He also claimed complete authority over men, either as Savior or as Judge. He even commanded the wind and the waves to obey Him, showing His sovereign power. (2) But our Lord did not exercise these three offices during the days of His earthly sojourn only. He also exercises them at this very hour from heaven. (a) By His Holy Spirit He has given us the inspired Scriptures. And He now applies these Scriptures to the hearts of men by the same Holy Spirit. (b) He also exercises His priestly office as He applies the benefits of His one sacrifice to the elect. He applies these benefits through the Word, and seals them by the sacraments. (c) And to Him now belongs all authority in heaven and earth. Thus He is subduing sinners to himself, and destroying the works of the devil. This work will continue until all enemies of Christ are put down, including death itself.

From this we can see why Christ becomes our Savior only in terms of these three offices. Man, by his fall, became ignorant, guilty, and sinful. He can be saved only when this ignorance is replaced by true knowledge; this guilt by righteousness; and this sinfulness by holiness. What, then, is necessary to the conversion of a lost sinner? (1) First, he must know something. He must know what none can teach him except Christ, by His Word and Spirit. He must know his own sin and misery, and the work of Jesus Christ as the only remedy. (2) He must feel his need for the cleansing blood of Christ. And he must feel that Christ's sacrifice is sufficient. (3) And he must cease to live a life of slavery to sin, by receiving Christ (resting upon Him alone for salvation as He is freely offered in the gospel). In other words, a man is saved only if, and when, Christ alone becomes his prophet, priest, and king.

Finally, we must see that Christ is with no Church that fails to acknowledge Him as the one prophet, priest, and king of the New Testament Church. No Church is perfect, of course, and some Churches are more faithful than others. But no Church is a true Church of Jesus Christ unless it has certain definite marks. These are: (1) the faithful preaching of the Word of God. This means that the doctrine taught in a true Church will always be according to the Bible, at least to such an extent that men will come to know their sin and misery and the work of Jesus Christ. "Churches" which teach other books (such as "the Book of Mormon," for example) are not true Churches because they do not faithfully teach the Word of God. Modernist "churches" are not true Churches because they deny (or at least neglect) central doctrines of the Bible. (2) A second mark of a true Church is the right administration of the sacraments. This means that such a Church will baptize believers and their children, and administer the Lord's Supper to such as profess the true religion and walk uprightly. We cannot call the Salvation Army a "true Church," in other words, because it does not administer the sacraments as Christ commanded. (3) A third mark of a true Church is the exercise of discipline. This means that the elders of the Church visit the members of the Church to warn them against false doctrine and wrong living. It means that when people persist in false doctrine or sinful habits, they are not allowed to continue as members of the Church. Only in such a Church—where all three of these are evident—can we say that Christ is truly present.

One of the most important things that we can learn from this part of the Catechism is that we must never separate these three offices. We must never neglect one while we honor another. In order to claim Jesus Christ as our Savior, for example, we must have our ignorance removed by His Word and Spirit, our guilt removed by His sacrificial blood, and our sinful desires brought more and more under His ruling power. Sometimes people think that they are Christians simply because they know certain doctrines. But knowledge alone is not conversion. Christ is not our prophet, priest, and king unless our feelings, and our will, are changed along with our knowledge. Sometimes people think that they are Christians because they have strong feelings (perhaps at a certain religious meeting, where a famous person is speaking). But feeling by itself is not conversion. There must also be knowledge, and a renewal of the will. Sometimes people think that they are Christians because they resolve "to turn over a new leaf." But an act of the will by itself is not conversion. There must first be true knowledge, and feeling, before there can be a renewal of the will into true conversion.

We see this same connection in the Church. Sometimes people think that they can have a true Church if they faithfully preach the gospel and administer the sacraments, *without* the proper exercise of discipline. We see this quite often today in some larger denominations where modernism (false doctrine) is rampant. People are allowed to remain members of the Church (and even ministers and elders of the Church) in spite of the fact that they deny essential truths of the gospel. Yet here and there we find a congregation where the minister tries to go on faithfully preaching the Word of God, and administering the sacraments. So some people remain, hoping that their particular congregation will remain faithful. However, what always happens in such instances in the long run is that the breakdown of any of these three marks (discipline, for example) causes the loss of all three. And when the whole denomination becomes unsound, *every* congregation suffers.

Questions:

1. Was Adam originally a prophet, priest, and king? Explain.
2. What was the consequence of the fall (as far as these offices are concerned)?
3. What does much of the Old Testament history center about?
4. Were the three offices separate in Abraham's day? At a later time?
5. Who was the first specially appointed prophet? Priest? King?
6 Were there successors in each of these offices? Were all faithful?
7. What did God accomplish through these Old Testament persons in these offices?
8. To whom did these three lines lead? Prove.
9. When did Christ fulfill these offices?
10. Must a sinner have Christ in all three offices to be saved? Why?
11. What are the marks of a true Church? Why are these necessary?

LESSON NINETEEN

Question 24. How doth Christ execute the office of a prophet?

Answer: Christ executeth the office of a prophet, in revealing to us,[1] by his word and Spirit,[2] the will of God for our salvation.[3]

1. No man hath seen God at any time: the only begotten Son, which is in the bosom of the Father, he hath declared him (John 1:18).

2. Which things also we speak, not in the words which man's wisdom teacheth, but which the Holy Ghost teachest . . . (I Cor. 2:13).

3. . . . from a child thou hast known the holy scriptures, which are able to make thee wise unto salvation . . . (II Tim. 3:15).

The Church, says Paul, was "built upon the foundation of the apostles and prophets, Jesus Christ himself being the chief corner stone" (Eph. 2:21). Just as the other foundation stones rest upon the chief cornerstone, so the apostles and prophets upon the Lord Jesus Christ. The Old Testament prophets were indeed authorized to speak for God. What they said, and wrote, was the very word of God. But it was not by their own power that they spoke. It was the Spirit of Christ that spoke through them. "The Spirit of Christ which was in them . . . testified beforehand the sufferings of Christ," says Peter (I Pet. 1:11). Then, when Christ came into the world, this revelation of God's Word came to its completion. Christ was himself the prophet promised by God. In Him, as Paul says, "are hid all the treasures of wisdom and knowledge" (Col. 2:3). It is for this reason that, with the death and resurrection of Christ, we move from the era of the prophetic word to that of the apostolic. By the prophetic we mean the Old Testament. It was, as a whole, the book of promise. The New Testament belongs to the realm of fulfillment. It is true, of course, that we read of prophets in the apostolic period. But they were only to fill the gap" (as it were) until the New Testament had been written. While it was being written they were able to supply inspired instruction which we now have in the Bible. Thus it is a mark of the "finished work" of Christ that there is no prophet or apostle in the

Church today. There could be prophets and apostles only so long as God's complete word had not been given. The prophets foretold what Christ would do. The apostles recorded what Christ did do.

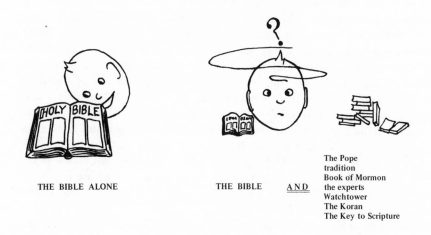

THE BIBLE ALONE   THE BIBLE   A N D

The Pope
tradition
Book of Mormon
the experts
Watchtower
The Koran
The Key to Scripture

Here we see a characteristic of false religion. False religion claims some other religious authority besides Christ speaking (by His Spirit) through the Bible. The Roman Catholic Church, for example, teaches the doctrine of apostolic succession. They say that the apostles transmitted their authority to successors. And they say that these successors (the popes) have power to speak God's Word. When the Pope speaks *ex cathedra* (from the chair of Peter, or, in other words, in his official capacity) he claims to speak without error. By this view, obviously, Christ did *not* complete divine revelation. He was not, on this view, the final prophet. With Him the succession of prophets did not come to an end. This is where the Church of Rome shows her apostasy. But we must notice that many modern cults manifest the same basic tendency to accept "new revelation" as part of their basis. Mormonism, for example, believes that Joseph Smith was a true prophet who came along 1800 years after Christ. In such religious movements as Seventh-day Adventism, Christian Science, and Jehovah's Witnesses we find this same tendency to add something to the Bible as the rule of faith and practice.

The historic Christian view is that Christ alone is the prophet of the Church, and that He now speaks to His Church through the Bible alone. This does not mean that human instruments are useless. To the contrary: "when he ascended up on high," says the Apostle, "he led captivity captive, and gave gifts unto men . . . he gave some, apostles; and some, prophets; and some, evangelists; and some, pastors and teachers" (Eph. 4:8, 11). Some of these offices were temporary (such as apostles and prophets). These, as we have seen, were needed only until the Bible was completed. But these other offices (evangelist, and teaching pastors) are a permanent gift of Christ to the Church. That is, Christ continues to call men to these offices today. But these men are not instruments of new revelation. No, it is not the task of these men to say something new. They are to "study to shew" themselves "approved unto God" as workmen that need "not to be ashamed, rightly dividing the word of truth" (II Tim. 2:15). Thus, the work of Christ—as the only prophet today in the Church—is accomplished, not by giving new revelation, but by giving men to study and proclaim the revelation that has already been given (namely, the Bible).

This might seem to make the work of ministers less profitable, and the people of God today to be in an inferior position. But the opposite is the case. Peter says that *"we have"* also a more sure word of prophecy" in the written Word of God, than *they* (the apostles, and others) *had* when they heard the voice of God from heaven. In other words, because the Bible is the Word of God written; because it is the complete Word of God; because it is clear and self-interpreting; and because the Holy Spirit has been given to enable God's elect people to understand the Bible; we are really more fully blessed by Christ's prophetic office than any of God's children in Old Testament times. We see this from what Jesus said concerning John the Baptist, the last of the prophets who were forerunners of Him. "Among them that are born of women there hath not risen a greater than John the Baptist: notwithstanding he that is least in the kingdom of heaven is greater than he" (Matt. 11:11). Even the humblest Christian today stands on a higher level of knowledge than John did, because of the fact that Christ now reveals the will of God to each believer directly through His Word and Spirit.

It is important to stress the fact that the foundation of true knowledge of God and of the way of salvation in Christ can come only directly from Christ by His Word and Spirit. This does not mean that there is no value in such things as the Creed, or the Confession, or the Catechism. These are summaries of the Christian faith written by uninspired men. They are valuable because (but only so far as) they are true to Scripture. They help us to learn more quickly what the Bible as a whole teaches. But it is only when we compare these with the Bible, and test and prove them by the Bible, that our knowledge is really sure. And it is only when we are enabled to do this by the Holy Spirit that we will be sure. As John says, "the anointing which ye have received of him abideth in you, and ye need not that any man teach you . . ." (I John 2:27). It is very important to stress this fact. For there is no other certainty or security for the believer. Some people say they accept what the Church says. Others say they accept what the minister says, or what some well-known or important professor teaches. Ohers say that they will go by what their parents believe to be true. Many people tend toward one or another of these sources, without ever realizing that they are going in the same direction as the Roman Catholic Church, or one of the false cults. But no one really has a certain and secure knowledge unless his reason for believing a certain thing to be true is that Christ has taught him in His Word.

At the time of the Reformation it was generally thought that ordinary people should not have the Bible. It was said that only scholars should study it, and only under careful supervision. Luther and other great Reformers, however, took the opposite view. They said that everyone should have the Bible. And they believed that unlearned people could understand what the Bible teaches (with the help of the Holy Spirit) better than the scholars who were unbelieving. In our modern age we are again seeing much of this old and false idea that only the scholars can understand the Bible. The fact of the matter is, however, that it has often been the scholars who have denied the Bible. It has often been the scholars who have led the Church away from the teaching of the Bible, and toward the false philosophies of the time. This does not mean that scholars are useless. But it does mean that no Christian should ever put anything above (or even on an equal level with) the Bible itself. Every Christian should always give supreme respect to what Christ says to him through the pages of the Bible. And the Bible should be read with the constant prayer that Christ might grant the gift of His Holy Spirit to enable one to understand it.

Blessed is that person who is sure—and rightly sure—that he knows what he believes. Blessed is that person who is able at all times to give a reason for the hope that is within him.

How shall the young direct their way? what light shall be their perfect
  guide?
Thy Word, O Lord, shall safely lead, if in its wisdom they confide.
Sincerely I have sought thee, Lord, O let me not from thee depart;
To know thy will and keep from sin, Thy Word I cherish in my
  heart (Ps. 119).

Questions:

1. In your own words explain what the apostle means in Ephesians 2:21.
2. Why did the prophetic word cease to be given after Christ had come?
3. Why were there prophets for a short time in the apostolic age?
4. What is the characteristic mark of true religion, shown in the illustration?
5. What is the characteristic mark of false religion, shown in the illustration?
6. What is meant by the doctrine of *apostolic succession?*
7. What is meant by the expression *ex cathedra?*
8. If Christ alone is the prophet of the Church, of what use are ministers
   now?
9. Are we in an inferior position because we receive the word of Christ in
   the Bible, rather than by living prophets and apostles? Prove and explain.
10. What value is there in Creeds, Confessions, and Catechisms?
11. What danger is there in these (and other) aids to faith?
12. Is it certain that wise scholars understand the Bible better than we
    do? Why?
13. What is the question asked in the Psalm version quoted above?
14. Put in your own words the answer which the Psalmist gives.

LESSON TWENTY

Question 25. How doth Christ execute the office of a priest?

Answer: Christ executeth the office of a priest, in his once offering up of himself a sacrifice to satisfy divine justice,[1] and reconcile us to God;[2] and in making continual intercession for us.[3]

1. Now of the things which we have spoken this is the sum: We have such an high priest . . . (Heb. 8:1). Christ was once offered to bear the sins of many (Heb. 9:28).

2. In all things . . . a merciful and faithful high priest in things pertaining to God, to make reconciliation for the sins of the people (Heb. 2:17).

3. He is able also to save them to the uttermost that come unto God by him, seeing he ever liveth to make intercession for them (Heb. 7:25).

We now come to consider the Reformed doctrine of "limited atonement," which is one of the most often misunderstood teachings of the Bible. The very use of the word "limited" with reference to the death of Jesus Christ offends some people. We can agree that this word is not the most desirable. It would be better to speak of "particular atonement." However, the word "limited" at least has the merit of drawing our attention to one of the most vital truths in all the Scripture. It is that Jesus Christ died as a substitute for *some* men, rather than for *all* men. He died to save His people from their sins (Matt. 1:21).

In order to grasp this distinctive teaching of the Reformed faith, it is necessary to see clearly that the atonement (or, sacrifice) of Jesus Christ is limited—not in its *value*, but in its *design*. The blood of Jesus is precious. It is far greater in value than any can measure. It is of unlimited value. And, however strange it may seem, the benefits of the death of Jesus Christ are freely offered to all who hear the gospel, whether they be elect or not. Yes, we can even say that if all men were to accept the offer of salvation made in the gospel, the value of Christ's sacrifice would still not be exhausted. Yet

95

there is still a limitation placed upon the atonement, by the design of the Father. It is this: those who *are* actually saved by the blood of Jesus Christ are those only whom it was the Father's intention to save by the death of His Son, and whom it was Christ's intention to save, by dying in their place. As Jesus himself said to the Father in His high-priestly prayer, "thou hast given him [i.e., the Son] power over all flesh, that he should give eternal life to as many as thou hast given him" (John 17:2). "Thine they were," said Jesus (speaking of His elect people), "and thou gavest them me" (John 17:6). "I lay down my life for the sheep," (John 10:15). "For I came down from heaven, not to do mine own will, but the will of him that sent me. And this is the Father's will which hath sent me, that of all which he hath given me I should lose nothing, but should raise it up again at the last day" (John 6:38, 39). And on the night in which He was betrayed, our Lord even said, "I pray not for the world, but for them which thou hast given me; for they are thine. And all mine are thine, and thine are mine" (John 17:9, 10). There can be no doubt that our Lord intended that the benefits of His death should be limited; limited, that is, to those whom the Father had given Him!

In contrast to this scriptural teaching, there have been two other views. One is the view that we may call *absolute universalism*. This view has been held by a denomination known as the Universalist Church. It teaches that God wills (or decrees) the salvation of all men—that Christ came to save all men— and that all men will be saved in the end. This view does at least have the merit of teaching that what actually happens is that which God planned (or decreed). It has the merit of saying that God the Father and the Lord Jesus Christ are working for the same goal, and that they reach the goal intended. But the Bible is so clear in teaching that some men will be lost forever, that no one can hold this view with even the appearance of taking the Bible as the truth of God (see Matt. 25:31-46, etc.). Consequently the doctrine of absolute universalism has always been rejected in the past by almost all who claim to be Christians. Before we turn from considering this view, however, it should be pointed out that this view is very strong today in modernist denominations, and in the World Council of Churches.

For those who want to accept the Bible as the Word of God there are two views that have been maintained. We now consider these two views. The one may be called *conditional universalism*. The other is *particularism*, which is simply another (and perhaps better) name for the Reformed doctrine of limited atonement. We illustrate these two views as follows:

96

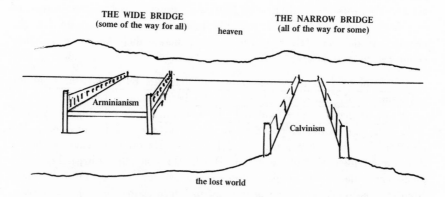

THE WIDE BRIDGE
(some of the way for all)

heaven

THE NARROW BRIDGE
(all of the way for some)

Arminianism

Calvinism

the lost world

Conditional universalism teaches that it is not God's will (decree) to save any particular person. Rather, according to this view, it was His will to partly save all men, leaving the other part of the saving to be performed by their own action. No man can be saved without Christ, in other words. But neither can Christ save any man without that person's own contribution. This "contribution" is usually said to be an act of man's free will, by which he (by his own power) repents and believes. This is like a great wide bridge— wide enough for everyone—but reaching only part way across a dangerous river. There is room for all, but only if they first swim out (by their own power) and climb up on the bridge. Now this view does seem attractive at first sight. It seems to make the salvation of all men possible. Yet, even those who hold this view admit that only some will be saved. So it is not really a gain to hold this view. The salvation that is supposed to be possible for *all*, is of actual benefit to only *some* And the terrible thing is that it is necessary to deny that Jesus Christ alone is the author of salvation, in order to gain this false appearance of "benefit for all."

The true doctrine, then, is the doctrine of *particularism*. This simply means that Jesus Christ offered himself as a substitute for certain particular people. This was the plan of the Father. He sent His Son to completely save some men (rather than to partly save all men). Just as the high priest, in the Old Testament, wore upon his breast "the names of the children of Israel" (Ex. 28:21) when he made the atonement in the Tabernacle, so Jesus Christ represented, not all men, but only His elect people. This is like a great bridge

97

that spans the whole river. It is not designed to carry all men part way across the raging torrent, but it is designed to carry some men all the way across. This is why the Bible calls Jesus the author, as well as the finisher, of our faith (Heb. 12:2). He not only paid the full debt of sin for His people, but also sent His Holy Spirit to regenerate their hearts so that they could repent and believe.

It is important to point out, however, that this particularism is, at the same time, truly universal. It is universal because Jesus Christ represented some out of every tongue and tribe and nation. It is for this reason that John says, "he is the propitiation for our sins: and not for ours only, but also for . . . the whole world" (I John 2:2). He does not say that Christ died for all men without exception. But he does say that Christ died for a great many men, from all the nations of the world, and not for just a few, from one nation only. Many people fail to interpret the Scriptures correctly, concerning the design (or the extent) of the death of Christ. This is because they do not see the difference between the kind of universalism (i.e., each and every person, without exception) the Bible does not teach, and the kind of universalism (i.e., some out of every tribe and nation) that the Bible does teach. And it is on the basis of this true universalism (which is also at the same time particular) that we can offer a complete salvation to all men, in the gospel. We can—and must—preach the gospel to every nation, because God has some in every nation for whom Christ died. We must call every individual to repent and believe the gospel, for no man knows which persons are written in the Lamb's book of life.

It is only when we maintain this doctrine of limited atonement that we can know the joy and certainty of salvation as we are taught to know it in the Bible. Paul says, "the Son of God . . . loved *me*, and gave himself for *me*" (Gal. 2:20). He could not say this if Christ had not died for him in particular, and as a personal substitute. This is, in fact, the heart of the matter. The believer says: "I have sinned. I am guilty. And I cannot be saved, unless there is someone willing and able to take my punishment, and to earn salvation for me. In order to save me, Christ rendered both active and passive obedience. In His active obedience, He obeyed all of God's commandments for me, as I ought to have done. In His passive obedience, He suffered all the punishment due unto me, in my place. And it is only because He really did do this, *for me*, that I can be sure that God will never cast me away from His presence." This is the heart of the particularism of the gospel.

Questions:

1. Is the word "limited" the best term to describe the death of Christ? Why?
2. What does the word "limited" mean in the phrase "limited atonement"?
3. To what does the word "limited" not refer in this phrase?
4. Cite a scripture verse or two proving the design of the atonement.
5. What is the teaching of "absolute universalism"?
6. Why is it that very few have held this teaching? What Church has held it?
7. What two views are illustrated in the drawing? Describe each briefly.
8. Why must "conditional universalism" be rejected?
9. What does "particularism" mean? How does the Old Testament priesthood show this?
10. Is there anything "universal" in the limited atonement? If so, what?
11. What does "the whole world" mean, in such texts as I John 2:2?
12. Does the doctrine of limited atonement hinder the gospel offer? Why?
13. Explain the "active" and "passive" obedience of Christ.
14. Why is the limited atonement necessary if we are to have assurance?

LESSON TWENTY-ONE

Question 26. How doth Christ execute the office of a king?

Answer: Christ executeth the office of a king, in subduing us to himself,[1] in ruling and defending us,[2] and in restraining and conquering all his and our enemies.[3]

1. Thy people shall be willing in the day of thy power (Ps. 110:3).

2. For the Lord is our judge, the Lord is our lawgiver, the Lord is our king: he will save us (Isa. 33:22). Behold, a king shall reign in righteousness . . . as the shadow of a great rock in a weary land (Isa. 32:1, 2).

3. For he must reign, till he hath put all enemies under his feet (I. Cor. 15:25).

When Jesus was crucified, these words were inscribed on the cross: "This is Jesus, the King of the Jews" (Matt. 27:37; but see also Mark 15:26; Luke 23:38; and John 19:19). No doubt wicked men intended this as mockery, but it was part of God's purpose and a testimony of the truth. This was foretold in Psalm 2. This Peter confirms in Acts 4:25. Thus when the dying thief cried, "Lord, remember me when thou comest into thy kingdom," Jesus replied, "Today shalt thou be with me in paradise" (Luke 23:42, 43). There is, in other words, a kingdom of which Jesus Christ is king. And it is to this great truth that this question of the Catechism directs our attention.

Let us notice, in the first place, then, that the kingly work of Jesus Christ is *a present spiritual activity.* And perhaps it will help to make this clear if we contrast the teaching of the Catechism with a rather popular modern error called dispensationalism. Most people who hold to dispensational teaching are orthodox when it comes to many fundamental doctrines of our faith. But they have fallen under the influence of an artificial system of Bible interpretation. This system divides Bible history into certain periods (or dispensations) in which it is said that God has had different ways of dealing with men. During the time of Moses, for example, it is said that God dealt with men according to law, whereas at the present He deals with men by grace. The truth is, of course, that God has always maintained the law *and* always dealt with sinners (since the fall) by grace as the only way of salvation. But the point of interest here is that, according to dispensationalists, Christ is *not yet king*. Dispensationalists say that He came to offer himself to the Jews as king, but when they refused, He delayed His kingdom. In the meantime God is saving men by the instrumentality of the Church. But when Christ comes again then He will establish His kingdom, and rule on earth for 1,000 years, much after the manner of present earthly kings, except for the moral perfection of His reign.

Against this teaching stands the clear teaching of Scripture. (1) The kingdom of Christ is already in existence. Paul says that when God has "delivered us from the power of darkness" He also "hath translated us into the kingdom of his dear Son" (Col. 1:13). (2) The kingdom of Christ is also spiritual and invisible. Jesus said, "my kingdom is not of this world" (John 18:36). "The kingdom of God cometh not with observation" (Luke 17:20). (3) It is a kingdom which will never end (Dan. 2:44; II Peter 1:11), although it will give way to a more perfect state of things at the end of the world (I Cor. 15:24). His kingdom is now being extended. It will then be complete. So the basic error of the dispensationalists is that they separate the kingdom of Jesus Christ from the Church.

We must notice, in the second place, however, that it is also an error to say that the kingdom is the Church. This is the great error of the Roman Catholic Church. According to this teaching, the Roman Catholic Church itself represents the kingdom of Christ in this world. That is why the effort is made to bring everything under the control of this Church. Every kind of organization and institution—schools, labor unions, political parties, etc.— should take orders from the Church. Only in this way, it is said, can Jesus Christ rule over all of life. He does this by means of His vicar, the Pope.

The Reformed view is this: while the Church and the kingdom of Jesus Christ are closely related, they are not identical. Christ is the king and head of the Church. But He also rules over a kingdom that includes much more than the Church. Thus it is the Reformed view that Christ should rule over every sphere of life, but not that the Church should exercise control over other organizations. The Church must indeed teach the Lord's people what the Bible has to say about Christian schools, labor relations, politics, etc., but then it is the responsibility of the people to work out these principles under the direct kingship of Christ. In each sphere (or circle of life activity), in other words, the believer is directly responsible to Christ. It is Christ himself who rules the hearts of His people by His word and Spirit. And it is by this direct rule of His people which He effects in all that they do that the kingdom of Christ exists in this world.

We illustrate these three different views as follows:

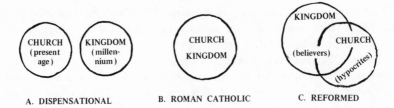

A. DISPENSATIONAL   B. ROMAN CATHOLIC   C. REFORMED

It will be observed that there are points of identity, and points of difference, in the Reformed view of the Church and kingdom. (1) They are the same in that: (a) Christ alone is king and head of both, (b) true believers alone belong to both (in a saving way), and (c) that one cannot *really* become a member of the one without, at the same time, becoming a member of the other. (2) They are different in that: (a) the Church has a distinct visible form, whereas the kingdom does not, (b) the Church has the keys to the kingdom (Matt. 16:19)—which is the power to admit men to, or exclude them from the kingdom by the preaching of the Word of God and the exercise of Church discipline—whereas the kingdom does not have keys to the Church, and (c) the Church concerns itself with a much "narrower" task than does the kingdom. As the Church preaches the Word of God, and administers discipline, it brings men into the kingdom. But when men are brought into the kingdom, they are then required (by the king, Jesus Christ) to order the whole of their lives by His authority. And it is this—the ordering of the whole of life under Christ's rule—that constitutes the kingdom. Wherever these believers go, whatever they do, they are to do all according to His will. He therefore exercises His rule (kingly authority) in and through them, in the world. It is this invisible, but real, exercise of His authority in the activities of His people in the world that brings His kingdom more and more into effect.

The Catechism not only says that Christ now executes the office of a king, it also speaks of His "restraining and conquering all his and our enemies." And the question naturally arises as to the future of His kingdom. When, in other words, can we expect to see "all enemies under his feet" (I Cor. 15:25)? In answer to this question three views have been held by Christians. In order to show these views we present the following diagram:

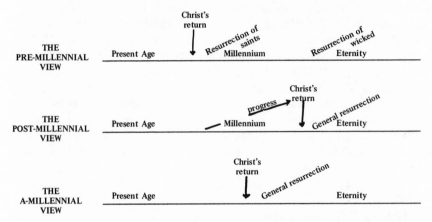

Pre-millennialists believe that Christ will return to resurrect the believers, and that He will then establish a kingdom which will endure for 1,000 years (the millennium). After this will come the resurrection of unbelievers, the judgment day, and then eternity. We do not agree with this view. It is important to note, however, that while all dispensationalists are pre-millennialists, not all pre-millennialists are dispensationalists. Pre-millennialists who are not dispensationalists admit that there is a present kingdom of Christ, as well as expecting a literal reign of Christ on earth, during the millennium. Post-millennialists believe that Christ will advance His present spiritual and invisible kingdom (through the work of the Church in preaching the gospel, etc.) until the whole world is evangelized. After this will follow an extended period (the millennium) in which righteousness and peace will cover the world. Then they believe that (perhaps after a great apostasy) Christ will return visibly, to raise all the dead, to judge the world, and usher in eternity. A-millennialists do not believe that the Bible promises any millennium. They believe that good and evil will both grow together until the harvest. They believe that one day Christ will return (without warning) and raise all the dead and bring them to judgment. After this follows the eternal state. The pre-millennialists are called pre-millennialists because they expect Christ's visible return before a millennial period. The post-millennialists are so named because they expect His return after a mil-

103

lennial period. The a-millennialists are called this because they do not expect a millennium.

We believe the a-millennial view is to be preferred for the following reasons: (1) the Scriptures say that no one can know when Christ will return (Acts 1:7; Matt 24:36ff.; I Tim. 5:1). This would not be so if men knew He would return after a millennium (1,000 years of peace). (2) The Scripture says that these are the last days (Heb. 1:2; John 6:39; 11:24; 12:48; Acts 2:17; II Tim. 3:1, etc.). If this be so, then we cannot expect a millennium after these days are ended by the coming of Christ. (3) In Christ's parable of the wheat and tares "both grow together until the harvest." This does not seem capable of agreement with the idea of a time of complete righteousness and peace before Christ returns. But let us remember that (apart from the dispensationalists) men may hold to any one of these three views and yet be considered orthodox Christians.

Questions:

1. Is Jesus Christ *now* a king? Prove.
2. What do dispensationalists teach about such doctrines as the birth of Christ?
3. What do they teach that is in error?
4. What are the three great principles that prove this to be wrong?
5. What is the great error of the Roman Catholic Church concerning the kingdom?
6. What is the difference between the Reformed and Roman Catholic view of the kingdom?
7. In the Reformed view, in what respects are the Church and kingdom identical?
8. In the Reformed view, in what respects are the Church and the kingdom different?
9. What does pre-millennialism teach? Post-millennialism? A-millennialism?
10. What are the arguments for the a-millennial view?
11. Can a person be orthodox and hold to any one of these views? Can a person be orthodox and hold to the dispensational view? Why?

LESSON TWENTY-TWO

Question 27. Wherein did Christ's humiliation consist?

Answer: Christ's humiliation consisted in his being born, and that in a low condition,[1] made under the law,[2] undergoing the miseries of this life,[3] the wrath of God,[4] and the cursed death of the cross,[5] in being buried,[6] and continuing under the power of death for a time.[7]

1. And she brought forth her first-born son, and wrapped him in swaddling clothes, and laid him in a manger (Luke 2:7).
2. God sent forth his son, made of a woman, made under the law (Gal. 4:4).
3. He is despised and rejected of men, a man of sorrows, and acquainted with grief (Isa. 53:3).
4. My God, my God, why hast thou forsaken me? [Jesus said] (Matt. 27:46).
5. He became obedient unto death, even the death of the cross (Phil. 2:8).
6. He was buried (I Cor. 15:4).
7. He rose again on the third day (I Cor. 15:4).

This question of the Catechism deals with a number of subjects that we have already considered. But there is good reason to see them in summary, for we need to realize that our Lord humbled himself exceedingly for our salvation. Here we see the "steps" by which our Savior "lowered himself to the depths" for us. Let us consider:

(1) It was an astounding thing that God should come into this world by taking unto himself a human nature. The late C. S. Lewis, the English writer, has made an apt comparison. He has said that this was like a shepherd becoming a lamb, in order to sacrifice himself to save the rest of the flock. Think what it would mean for a human being to lower himself to such a position. Yet Christ lowered himself even more in order to save us. This is true because there is a far greater difference between God and man than there is between man and beast. (2) We also need to remember that when Christ did become man, He did not come to occupy the highest and best position among

105

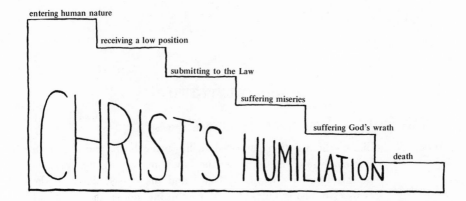

entering human nature

receiving a low position

submitting to the Law

suffering miseries

suffering God's wrath

CHRIST'S HUMILIATION death

men. He was not born in a king's palace. He did not have wealth and social standing among men. His mother, and Joseph, who was to Him as a human father, were poor people. They were living in hard times when the Roman soldiers occupied their country. (3) And even though our Lord Jesus Christ as God was the giver of the law, or, in other words, the one who stood above that law which He had given, yet when He became man He himself was subject to that law. When He became a man it was His duty to keep the commandments of God perfectly, just as it is the duty of all other men. And we must remember that He too was tempted in all points just as we are. He too lived in a world full of temptation. And strange as it may seem, it was a terribly difficult thing for Him to keep all the commandments of God continually. (4) The Bible tells us that Jesus experienced the misery that we experience (except for the misery of feeling guilty when we have done wrong). He knew hunger, pain, sorrow, and poverty. He knew what it was like to be unjustly hated, and ridiculed. He has "borne our griefs, and carried our sorrows" says the prophet Isaiah (53:4) He was subject, in other words, to all the effects of the fall of man, except that He was sinless. (5) This suffering came to full expression when Jesus suffered the full consequences of sin in becoming subject to the wrath of God. When Jesus cried out, "My God, my God, why has thou forsaken me?" He was actually experiencing the same kind of thing that the lost will experience on the judgment day. Then they who have not Christ as their Savior will be cast out of God's presence. They will go into "outer darkness." There will be weeping and wailing and gnashing of teeth. But our Lord himself was "made a curse for us: for it is written, cursed is every one that hangeth on a tree" (Gal. 3:13). (6) And Christ paid

106

the penalty for sin in full when He died the cruel death of the cross. "For he [God] hath made him [Jesus] to be sin for us, who knew no sin; that we might be made the righteousness of God in him" (II Cor. 5:21). When the Apostles' Creed says "he descended into hell," we are not to think that Christ went to hell, as lost sinners do, *after* death. The correct interpretation of this phrase in the Creed is this: Christ suffered the pains of hell in His death on the cross. And He remained subject to the power of death for a time just as all believers who share in the benefits of His death.

We must realize that our Lord did this voluntarily. When *we* were born into this world, it is not because we choose to be born. We have nothing to say about when, or where, or to which parents, we will be born. But with Jesus it was different. For long before His birth He spoke (through His prophets) to promise that He would come. "Then said I, Lo, I am come: in the volume of the book, it is written of me" (Ps. 40:7). So *He* did choose when, where, and how He would be born. And that is why we must speak of His great "humiliation." Says the Apostle:

> Let this mind be in you which was also in Christ Jesus: who, being in the form of God, thought it not robbery to be equal with God: but made himself of no reputation, and took upon him the form of a servant, and was made in the likeness of men: and being found in fashion as a man, he humbled himself, and became obedient unto death, even the death of the cross [Phil. 2:5-8].

When the Apostle says that Christ was originally "in the form of God," he simply means that Christ was "the same in substance" with the Father and the Holy Spirit, and "equal in power and glory." In other words, Jesus was just God, and it was therefore no robbery for Him to claim equality with God because there is no robbery involved in claiming something that already belongs to a person. But Christ was unmindful of these things. He was rather mindful of the dire need of His elect people. And so He entered upon His great humiliation.

It is necessary to make quite clear, however, that when Jesus did this (became man), He did not in doing it cease to be God. He did not, in His estate of humiliation, cease to be "the same in substance" and equal "in power and glory" with respect to the Father and the Holy Spirit. Some have seriously erred in teaching this wrong view. This teaching is called the *kenosis* doctrine. The Greek word *kenosis* is found in Philippians 2:7, and is sometimes translated (as in the Revised Standard Version) as "emptied." Those who prefer this translation sometimes say that Jesus *emptied* himself

107

of His divine attributes. They say He left His divine nature, as it were, or at least His divine powers, when He became man. We could well say that, according to this false view, Christ's humiliation meant the subtraction of His deity.

But the true view is that Christ's humiliation consisted—not in the fact that His divine nature, or attributes, were *subtracted* from Him—but in the fact that a true human nature was *added* to Him. There are a number of reasons why this false kenosis doctrine must be rejected. (1) It must be rejected because it would suggest the idea that Christ's divine nature was changeable. But God is unchangeable. (2) It must be rejected because the Scripture clearly teaches that Jesus was God even in His estate of humiliation. "That holy thing which shall be born of thee shall be called the Son of God," said the angel (Luke 1:35). (3) It must be rejected because it does not solve the "mystery" of the incarnation. We cannot fully understand the astounding fact that the second person of the Godhead, without any diminution of His divine attributes, became a real man. But this theory does not help to explain that mystery. It only makes it more unintelligible.

While our Lord's humiliation did not involve any subtraction of deity, it did involve what we may perhaps call a "veiling" of His deity, for a time. It is quite evident, from the Bible, that many people who saw Jesus did not—from that fact alone—realize that He was God. Neither did Jesus manifest His divine power and glory until He entered upon His public and official work as the Messiah. "This beginning of miracles did Jesus in Cana of Galilee," says John, "and manifested forth his glory, and his disciples believed on him" (John 2:11). It was only because our Lord did such mighty works that men could "behold his glory, the glory as of the only begotten of the Father" (John 1:14). His miracles were a demonstration of the fact that He *did* possess the attributes of deity in the higest sense. Yet even so, the Bible seems to allow for the fact that Christ's divine nature was—for the time then present (or during His humiliation)—somewhat obscured. Jesus said, "all manner of sin and blasphemy shall be forgiven unto men: but the blasphemy against . . .the Holy Ghost, it shall not be forgiven him, neither in this world, neither in the world to come" (Matt. 12:31, 32). Since Jesus is God, just as the Holy Spirit is, there must be a reason why the mercy of God is such that blasphemy against (speaking against) Jesus may be forgiven, whereas blasphemy against the Holy Spirit is not forgivable. We believe that the one thing which accounts for this difference is the fact that Jesus is not only God, but also man. And, since His divine nature was veiled, so to speak, during the time

108

of His humiliation, this must be the reason why blasphemy against Him—
terrible as it was—was forgivable.

Someone has expressed the mystery of Christ's humiliation in these words,
with which we conclude our discussion of this important subject. "Remaining what He was, He became what He was not." He who understands—and
remembers—this sentence will know how to avoid most of the errors that
have arisen in the history of the Church with respect to the humiliation of
Jesus.

Questions:

1. Why does the Catechism repeat here what has (in part) been said before?
2. After reading the lesson write a brief phrase for each of the six steps
   in Christ's humiliation.
3. With what does C. S. Lewis compare Christ's coming into human nature?
4. Why was it a humiliation for Christ to be "made under the law"?
5. What were some of the miseries Christ experienced?
6. With what could Christ's experience of God's wrath be compared?
7. What is the correct interpretation of the phrase, "he descended into
   hell"?
8. What does "being in the form of God" mean, in Philippians 2:6?
9. Why was it not "robbery" for Christ to be equal with God?
10. What is the error of the so-called "kenosis" theory?
11. What is the true meaning of the word "kenosis" in contrast to this
    theory?
12. What reasons can be given to prove the kenosis theory wrong?
13. Was the divine nature of Christ manifested during the time of His
    humiliation? Explain.
14. Is *all* blasphemy wrong? What is blasphemy?
15. Why is blasphemy against Jesus Christ forgivable?
16. Write, from memory, the sentence beginning: "Remaining what . . .
    etc."

LESSON TWENTY-THREE

Question 28. Wherein consisteth Christ's exaltation?

Answer: Christ's exaltation consisteth in his rising again from the dead on the third day,[1] in ascending up into heaven,[2] in sitting at the right hand of God the Father,[3] and in coming to judge the world at the last day.[4]

1. He rose again the third day according to the scriptures (I Cor. 15:4).

2. . . . he was taken up; and a cloud received him out of their sight (Acts 1:9).

3. . . . he raised him from the dead, and set him at his own right hand in the heavenly places (Eph. 1:20).

4. This same Jesus . . . shall so come in like manner as ye have seen him go into heaven (Acts 1:11). . . . he hath appointed a day, in the which he will judge the world in righteousness by that man whom he hath ordained . . . (Acts 17:31).

When our Lord was about to finish the work that He came to do on earth, He said, "And now, O Father, glorify thou me with thine own self with the glory which I had with thee before the world was" (John 17:5). It is to this that the Catechism now directs our attention, as it sets before us the "steps" involved in Christ's exaltation.

110

(1) There was, first of all, our Lord's resurrection. The body which rose from the grave was the *same* body that had before been crucified and buried. It was different in quality. But it was the same in identity. Nothing is more certain from the testimony of Scripture than this. It was not (as some have said) a mere vision that the disciples imagined that they saw. When the disciples saw Jesus, "they were terrified and affrighted, and supposed that they had seen a spirit. And he said unto them, Why are ye troubled? and why do thoughts arise in your hearts? Behold my hands and my feet, that it is I myself: handle me, and see: for a spirit hath not flesh and bones, as ye see me have" (Luke 24:37-39). A number of different attempts have been made to explain what happened, without accepting the testimony of the Bible. Some have suggested that the disciples believed so strongly that Jesus would rise again from the dead, that they imagined things accordingly. But the Bible clearly records the fact that they did *not* expect it. In fact, they could hardly believe it even when it actually happened. Others have suggested that the disciples deliberately lied, thus spreading the story that Jesus had risen from the dead in order to keep their movement going. But this becomes preposterous when we remember that the disciples were willing to die rather than to deny that Jesus rose from the dead. Some say that they just cannot believe "the story of the miracle." But the trouble is, that they must then decide what to do with the "miracle of the story." That is, they are left with the insoluble problem of how such a sober story could ever have been written. The story is either true, or else it is the product of insanity or wickedness. And, after nearly two thousand years, no one has been able to show that it comes from either insane or wicked men. No satisfactory explanation has come forth except to believe that it actually did happen.

(2) After a period of forty days, during which our Lord frequently met with His disciples, He was then received up into glory. "And while they looked stedfastly toward heaven, as He went up, behold, two men stood by them in white apparel; which also said, Ye men of Galilee, why stand ye gazing up into heaven? this same Jesus, which is taken up from you into heaven, shall so come in like manner as ye have seen him go into heaven" (Acts 1:10, 11). This is another element of "the story" that makes it impossible for unbelievers to devise their own explanations. For if these "appearances" were only imaginary, or visionary, why should they suddenly terminate after forty days? Some modernists today scoff at the idea of Jesus going "up into heaven." Heaven, they say, is not "up there," for we now know (as they supposedly did not know in Bible times) that the world

is round. The real difficulty for such people, however, is simply this: they do not believe that Christ ever rose from His grave in the same body in which He was crucified. They therefore cannot believe that He ascended up from the earth in the sight of men. But that is exactly what the historic Christian faith teaches. Let us put it precisely. At a certain moment of time, at a certain location, the flesh and bones (and, of course, the soul) of Jesus were lifted up from this world, just as truly as when one of our modern astronauts goes up from the surface of the earth. And when it happened the earth was actually lighter by just so many pounds. If a photographer had been present, pictures could have been taken, just as in the case of any other real event.

(3) Our Lord now sits at the right hand of the Father. This, of course, is a figurative description. For God does not have bodily parts. The right hand of the Father is simply "the place of honor," "God also hath highly exalted him, and given him a name which is above every name: that at the name of Jesus every knee should bow" (Phil. 2:9, 10). We may wonder why the Bible speaks of God giving this to Jesus, since it belonged to Him as God before He came to the world. The reason is that when Jesus returned to the Father, He was not only God, but also man. And because He was also man, He could receive this honor only as God conferred it. However, let it be observed that the honor given is very great. Christ (the God-man) now has a name which is above every name. This means that He is to be honored as the Father himself and the Holy Spirit are honored. Thus we can now say that there is a man to whom belongs all the glory and to whom must be given all the honor that belongs to God, because this man *is* also God. We cannot say just *where* Jesus is at this time. But we do know that He *is located* at a particular place. This is denied by Roman Catholics and Lutherans. They teach (in different ways) that the human nature of Christ is present on earth at many different places at the same time (during the administration of the sacrament of the Lord's Supper). This is really a denial of the true human nature of Christ, for an omnipresent nature is not really human. The Bible, moreover, says that Jesus is one "whom the heaven must receive until the times of restitution of all things" (Acts 3:21). Christ is present with us now in the person of the Holy Spirit. But one day He is coming again in the same visible human body as the disciples saw when He ascended.

(4) Christ is coming to judge the world at the last day. In order to set forth the Scripture teaching concerning this event, let us consider the follow-

ing points. (a) "Of that day and hour knoweth no man" (Matt. 24:36). Our Lord himself did not know when it would be, during His earthly ministry (Mark 13:32). We must always be careful, therefore, that we be not misled by any who seek to deceive us. "It is not for you to know the times or the seasons, which the Father hath put in his own power," said Jesus to His disciples (Acts 1:7). (b) It follows from this that there will be no *signs* whereby the time of His coming can be known beforehand. Many have thought that the events mentioned in Matthew 24:5-35 will occur near the time of His coming so that this time might be predicted at least in a general way. But Jesus said that the generation living when these words were spoken would not pass away until all things were fulfilled (Matt. 24:34). We hold that these things did happen in that generation. And since the coming of Christ is compared, in our Lord's teaching, to the flood of Noah, the thief in the night, and the lightning that shines from the east to the west, we believe it is an error to look for signs that will indicate the time of His return. If anything, it would seem that Christ will come just when people feel safe because they see no "signs." "For when they shall say peace and safety; then sudden destruction cometh upon them" (I Thess. 5:3). (c) The coming of Christ will be sudden. (d) It will be public. People will see it with their own eyes. (e) At the time of His return all the dead will be raised up from their graves (John 5:28). (f) Those who are alive when Jesus comes will be instantly changed (I Thess. 4:17; I Cor. 5:10). (i) And the Lord will then separate the human race into two companies, the saved and the lost.

It is important to note, in conclusion, that Christ is just as active now, in His estate of exaltation (on behalf of His people) as He was in His estate of humiliation. Christ did not leave the earth for His own sake. He went to prepare a place for us (John 14:3). He now makes intercession for His people (Heb. 7:25). From heaven He continues His conquest of all His and our enemies. "For he must reign, till he hath put all enemies under his feet. The last enemy that shall be destroyed is death . . . then cometh the end, when he shall have delivered up the kingdom to God, even the Father; when he shall have put down all rule and all authority and power" (I Cor. 15:25, 26, 24). We see, then, that the day of Christ's present mediation will end. Then we will enjoy a communion with God that is more direct than that which we now know. But Christ's exaltation will never end. It will simply be that we shall be like Him when we see Him as He is. But "every man in his own order; Christ the firstfruits; afterward they that are Christ's at his coming" (I Cor. 15:23).

Questions:

1. What are the steps of Christ's exaltation?
2. With what body did Christ arise? Explain.
3. What are some of the "theories" that men have invented to explain this away?
4. To what charge against the disciples do such theories lead?
5. Why do such theories always fail?
6. Give a reason why this story cannot be a product of insanity?
7. Give a reason why this story cannot be a product of wickedness.
8. Why do modernists object to speaking of heaven as "up there"?
9. Did the body (and soul) of Jesus actually go "up"? Prove.
10. Are we to take literally the words: "sitteth at the right hand of God the Father"? Why?
11. If Christ is God, how can we explain that He was exalted to a place of of honor?
12. What error is taught by Roman Catholics and Lutherans (although in two different ways) concerning the human nature of Christ?
13. What will be the order of events when Christ comes again? (Try to write as many as you can, in order, from memory.)
14. Can "that day" be predicted as to time? Why?
15. Christ compares His coming to the days of Noah, the thief, and the lightning. What does this show us.
16. Why did Christ enter upon His present estate of exaltation?
17. What are some of Christ's present activities on behalf of His people?
18. Will Christ always stand as mediator between God and man as He now stands? Why?

LESSON TWENTY-FOUR

Question 29. How are we made partakers of the redemption purchased by Christ?

Answer: We are made partakers of the redemption purchased by Christ by the effectual application of it to us[1] by his Holy Spirit.[2]

1. But as many as received him, to them gave he power to become the sons of God, even to them that believe on his name (John 1:12).

2. Not by works of righteousness which we have done, but according to his mercy he saved us, by the washing of regeneration, and renewing of the Holy Ghost (Tit. 3:5).

The *only* redeemer of God's elect is the Lord Jesus. This is true not only because He accomplished our redemption (in His messianic work as prophet, priest, and king). It is also true because He applies this redemption to His elect by the operation of His Spirit. This does not mean that the Holy Spirit is a mere force or power. No, the Holy Spirit is a person. He is equal with the Father and the Son in power and glory. And He is of the same substance, or essence, with them. Our salvation, in other words, is a consequence of the mighty power and grace of the three persons of the Godhead, and not of Jesus only. We must understand that the doctrine of the Trinity is basic to an understanding of the doctrine of salvation. God the Father has given His Son to be the redeemer of His elect. Christ the Son has purchased redemption by His active and passive obedience. The Holy Spirit applies redemption in the experience of the elect. Every system of teaching which claims to be Christian can therefore be judged according to its faithfulness (or lack of faithfulness) to the honor and glory of the triune God. (The student is to consult the Appendix, Diagram C.)

Modernism has had various names in the history of the Christian Church. In New England history it was called Unitarianism. In the Reformation era it was called Socinianism. And in the ancient Church the word for this basic type of teaching was Pelagianism. Of course, there are differences. Modern-

115

ism is not exactly the same as Unitarianism, Socinianism, or Pelagianism. But the basic view of the way of salvation is the same in these different systems of thought. These are all just variations of the same naturalistic view. We say "naturalistic" because what is believed by those who hold to these views is this: there is no need for the supernatural, or miraculous. When one subtracts from the gospel the doctrine of Christ's virgin birth, bodily resurrection, etc., all that is left is a merely human Jesus who sets an example for others. The power which actually saves men, however, comes out of themselves. Man becomes his own savior.

Another view which has had many manifestations in history we now call *Arminianism*. James Arminius, who died in 1609, taught that the salvation of sinners depended partly upon God and partly upon man. He taught that sinners depend upon God the Father, who gave Jesus Christ to die for them; and upon Jesus Christ, who gave himself as a sacrifice for sin. But he did not believe that sinners depend upon the Holy Spirit alone for the regeneration of the soul. Arminianism, then, has become the common name for the system of teaching that fails to recognize the work of the Holy Spirit in a proper manner. And whenever there is this failure, it tends to work against a proper recognition of God throughout the entire system. This is seen quite clearly in the Roman Catholic type of teaching. In the Roman Catholic system God cannot save man without man's cooperation (in the use of the sacraments) just as man cannot save himself without God's cooperation. The effect of this compromise is seen quite clearly in the whole Roman Catholic system. It is the great "and" religion: faith *and* works, Christ *and* Mary, etc.

But the Reformed faith (or, *Calvinism*) teaches a consistent supernaturalist view of salvation. Again, this view has had different names in history. It was, for example, called Augustinianism because it was faithfully taught by the great theologian Augustine in the ancient Catholic Church. It was recovered at the time of the Reformation by all of the great reformers such as Luther, Zwingli, Knox, and Calvin. It is called Calvinism today simply because Calvin was the one who gave that teaching the clearest and most convincing expression. It is the system that matters, however, and not the man who teaches it, or his name. The system matters because it teaches that sinful man is completely dependent upon God for salvation. And this is just as true when it comes to the application of this redemption as it is in the planning, or accomplishing of it. "For of him," says Paul, "and through him, and to him, are all things: to whom be glory for ever. Amen" (Rom. 11:36).

As we consider the next few questions of the Catechism, we will take up the various "steps" in the application of redemption. But here let us get firmly fixed in our memory what these steps are. (Keep in mind that these steps give us the *logical* order. It is not to be thought that there is necessarily a passage of time between these successive steps. Some of them at least, occur at virtually the same time.) The steps are:

1—*Effectual Calling*—(which is composed of two elements)
  (A) Calling—the gospel is preached to sinners without distinction, and salvation is freely offered to all
  (B) Regeneration—only when the Holy Spirit creates a new nature in a sinner is he able to "hear" the gospel in a saving way (like sight given to the blind enables light to enter)
2—*Conversion*—the turning of a sinner unto Christ (also two elements)
  (A) Repentance—the whole man turning away from sin
  (B) Faith—the whole man turning unto Jesus Christ
3—*Justification*—when a sinner trusts in Christ, he is at once (and forever) accepted as righteous
4—*Adoption*—when a sinner trusts in Christ and is justified, he is also incorporated into God's family
5—*Sanctification*—from conversion until death the Holy Spirit enables a believer to fight against sin and for holiness
6—*Glorification*—at the last day, when Christ returns, believers will be made perfect in body and soul

You will note that there is really no place for anything more than a mere semblance of the above "steps" in the modernist view of things. The modernist might indeed speak of the need of "conversion." But he would mean only that it is up to the sinner to "make a new start" in life by "turning over a new leaf" strictly by his own will and power. And if the modernist were to speak of the need for sanctification, he would mean only that a man who has "turned over a new leaf" should try to keep going onward and upward. But there is no place at all for the work of the Holy Spirit as the necessary first enabling act. It simply is not admitted that sinful man can do nothing as respects salvation by his own natural power. In the Arminian view (and other views that resemble it) there is much more of the appearance of these "steps." Arminians do speak of the work of the Holy Spirit as if it were essential to the salvation of sinners. But in spite of this appearance, the Arminian view is also quite unacceptable. For the Arminian view teaches that the activity of the sinner himself must precede that of the Holy Spirit, and prepare the way

117

for His coming into the heart. In other words, according to this view, it is not the Holy Spirit who enables the sinner to repent and believe in Christ. It is rather the sinner who allows the Holy Spirit to regenerate his soul because he repents and believes. (In the Arminian view, man first repents and believes, and then—after that—is regenerated by the Holy Spirit.) It is not the Holy Spirit who enables man to do what needs to be done. It is rather man who enables the Holy Spirit to do what needs to be done. The contrast between the Reformed and Arminian views can be seen very vividly in the explanation that is given for a certain scripture text. "Behold, I stand at the door and knock," says Jesus, "if any man hear my voice, and open the door, I will come in to him" (Rev. 3:20). The Arminian says, in effect, that this is the Holy Spirit asking to come into the sinner's heart, and that the sinner must open his own heart by his own natural power, so that the Holy Spirit can come in and regenerate the soul. The Reformed view, on the other hand, is that it is Christ who asks to come in (and this *is* what the book of Revelation actually says). But it is the Holy Spirit who gives the sinner the ability to open the door. The sinner, by nature, is dead in trespasses and sins. He cannot hear the voice of Christ with the will and desire to let Him come in. But when the Holy Spirit works the miracle of regeneration, the dead sinner is made alive. Then he wants to open the door and let Christ come in. By this view it is the Holy Spirit who does the decisive thing. For it is only after He has performed the great work of regeneration that the sinner can do what this verse of scripture requires.

The Reformed view, then, is as follows. A sinner dead in trespasses and sins hears the gospel preached. He is invited to come to Christ. But he does not want this. He fights against it. Then, when the Holy Spirit wills to do so, He enters into that sinner's heart and regenerates him. Suddenly the sinner begins to hate sin and to want Christ. He repents and believes. Then he is instantly justified and adopted. From that time on, during the rest of his life, he holds fast to Jesus and strives to live with and for Him. Finally, on that last great day, he is raised up from the dead and made like unto Christ in both body and soul. And the one thing that he will want to say to all eternity is that the praise belongs to God alone. For he will not owe any of his salvation to himself!

Questions:

1. With what person of the Godhead are we particularly concerned in this lesson?

118

what does this mean?

2. Is the Holy Spirit a power or force?
3. By what can every system of teaching claiming to be Christian be judged?
4. What is another name that has been given to the type of teaching now called Modernism?
5. To whom does Modernism teach men to look for salvation?
6. After whom is Arminianism named?
7. What person of the Godhead receives completely inadequate account in the teaching of Arminianism?
8. To whom does Arminianism teach men to look for salvation?
9. What other system of teaching resembles Arminianism in this?
10. Is Calvinism (or, the Reformed faith) something that originated at the time of the Reformation? Explain.
11. To whom does the Reformed Christian look for salvation?
12. What are the steps in the application of redemption?
13. Are any of these steps found in Modernism? Explain.
14. How would an Arminian have to rearrange these steps?
15. How do Arminians explain Revelation 3:20? How do Calvinists explain it?
16. Be able to summarize in your own words the last paragraph of the lesson.

LESSON TWENTY-FIVE

Question 30. How doth the Spirit apply to us the redemption purchased by Christ?

Answer: The Spirit applieth to us the redemption purchased by Christ,[1] by working faith in us,[2] and thereby uniting us to Christ in our effectual calling.[3]

Question 31. What is effectual calling?

Answer: Effectual calling is the work of God's Spirit,[4] whereby, convincing us of our sin and misery,[5] enlightening our minds in the knowledge of Christ,[6] and renewing our wills,[7] he doth persuade and enable us to embrace Jesus Christ freely offered to us in the gospel.[8]

1. It is the Spirit that quickeneth; the flesh profiteth nothing (John 6:63).

2. By grace are ye saved through faith: and that not of yourselves; it is the gift of God (Eph. 2:8).

3. God is faithful, by whom ye were called into the fellowship of his Son Jesus Christ our Lord (I Cor. 1:9).

4. . . . God; who hath saved us, and called us with an holy calling (II Tim. 1:8, 9).

5. Now when they heard this, they were pricked in their hearts, and said . . . what shall we do? (Acts 2:37).

6. To open their eyes, and to turn them from darkness to light, and from the power of Satan unto God (Acts 26:18).

7. And I will give them one heart, and I will put a new spirit within you . . . (Ezek. 11:19).

8. No man can come to me, except the Father which hath sent me draw him (John 6:44).

God has decided to bring sinners to salvation through the preaching of the gospel. "It pleased God by the foolishness of preaching to save them that believe," says the Apostle (I Cor. 1:21). It is for this reason that Christ gave His Church the task of going into all the world to preach the gospel to every man (Matt. 28:19, 20, etc.). Except for infants who die in infancy, and mentally retarded persons who are not capable of grasping the significance of words, this is the way in which men must be saved. For "faith cometh by hearing, and hearing by the word of God" (Rom. 10:17). And "the gospel of Christ . . . is the power of God unto salvation to every one that believeth" (Rom. 1:16).

But the great question is: Why do some men accept the gospel when they hear it, while others do not? Why does the gospel bring some men to conversion, while others are only hardened? In answer to this question, we must first understand that the reason is not in the gospel itself. It is the same gospel that is preached to one man as is preached to the other. Jesus Christ is freely offered in the gospel to all sinners without exception. Some have supposed that salvation is really offered only to "the elect." "God," they say, "only intends to save the elect, and so it follows that God can offer salvation to them only. If God offered it to the others it would not be sincere." But however reasonable this may seem to the mind of man, it is not true. For "whosoever shall call upon the name of the Lord shall be saved" (Rom. 10:13). There is nothing in the gospel which prevents any man from accepting the offer of salvation contained in it.

A second thing that we must understand is that the reason for this difference between men is not something that finds its source in them. If one man accepts the gospel and another man does not, we might imagine that the one man had a better nature than the other. We might imagine that the one was more sinful by nature than the other. But this, again, is not true. The Bible tells us that all men are by nature dead in trespasses and sins (Eph. 2:1). And there is no man who will ever accept the gospel of his own natural will and desire. "The natural man receiveth not the things of the Spirit of God: for they are foolishness unto him: neither can he know them" (I Cor. 2:14). The simple truth is, then, that if God were to leave men to their own power, and to their own natural desire, no man on earth would ever accept the gospel.

And yet, as we know, some men do accept the gospel! So again we ask the question: Why do some men accept the gospel offer? The answer is that some are *effectually* called. And they are effectually called because they not only hear the true gospel preached, but also are regenerated by the Holy Spirit. This process we may outline as follows: (1) The gospel is preached

121

to a group of persons. All who hear the gospel are dead in sin. They cannot believe it because they consider it to be foolish. (2) Then, in the case of some, the Holy Spirit performs a mighty work. It is called "quickening" (Eph. 2:5), "creating" (2:10), "being born again" (John 3:4, 7), and being "raised up from the dead" (Eph. 2:6). It is a miracle which restores man spiritually, as much as the miracles of Christ during His earthly ministry restored physical ability to the blind, deaf, lame, etc. (3) In such cases, the result of this regenerating work of the Holy Spirit is this: the gospel has a powerful effect. What before seemed foolishness now pricks the heart (Acts 2:37). And what before seemed only as the word of men is now received "as it is in truth, the word of God, which effectually worketh" in them "that believe" (I Thess. 2:13). Let us illustrate:

Figure A. CALLING (only)

Figure B. EFFECTUAL CALLING

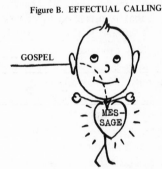

GOSPEL in one ear

MESSAGE out the other

GOSPEL

MES-SAGE

"the natural man receiveth not the things of the Spirit . . ."

I Cor. 2:14

". . . but God hath revealed them unto us by his Spirit . . ."

I Cor. 2:10

What effectual calling means can perhaps be seen more readily if we compare it with the raising of Lazarus from the dead (John 11). Lazarus was dead. He was not able to hear anything, or do anything, because he was dead. Yet our Lord Jesus Christ walked up to his grave and said, "Lazarus, come forth." This is similar to what we see (Fig. A, above) when a sinner hears the gospel. It "goes in one ear and out the other" because he is spiritually dead. But how different it is when the Holy Spirit regenerates the heart (Fig. B). Just as our Lord gave Lazarus the power to hear His voice, so the Holy Spirit gives sinners the ability to hear and obey the gospel.

It is sometimes said that this doctrine makes men little more than pawns on a chessboard. It is said that those who do not receive the regeneration of the Holy Spirit cannot be saved even if they want to be saved. And it is said that when a man does receive the Holy Spirit, he will be saved even if he does not want to be saved. Or, in other words, this teaching is said to leave no real place for man's own will: man can be lost against his own will, and saved against his own will! But this is not true. (1) It is not true, in the first place, because no man is "lost against his own will." As we have already seen, "the natural man receiveth not the things of the Spirit." Man does not want to be saved in the way that God requires. It is not his will to accept salvation through Jesus Christ alone. And it simply is not fair to blame this on God. God has not made man this way. God has not forced man to feel this way. (2) It is not true, in the second place, because regeneration is not an act of *coercion* (forcing man to act against his will) but rather an act of *creation* (creating in man a new will). When we speak of this as a work of *irresistible grace* we do not mean that God makes people do what they don't want to do. What we mean is that God changes people so that they want to do what they did not want to do before.

When a man has been regenerated by the Holy Spirit three things are bound to follow. (1) Such a person will see the truth of the gospel. As a blind man whose sight has been restored will see the beauty of the sunset, so this man will be able to see the gospel for what it is. (2) He will also feel a deep conviction as to his own unworthiness and guilt before God. He will feel his need of Jesus as his substitute who died to pay the price of his sin. This will not be something forced upon him. It will rather be something that he feels because his renewed nature wants to act this way. (3) Therefore he will repent of his sin and believe on the Lord Jesus Christ. He will want to do this because he now realizes his own need, and that the work of Jesus Christ is the only remedy there is for that need. Thus the work of the Holy Spirit is not to force men to be saved, but "to open their eyes, and to turn them from darkness to light, and from the power of Satan unto God, that they may receive forgiveness of sins, and inheritance among them which are sanctified by faith" (see Acts 26:18).

In conclusion, let us note that there are two dangers to be avoided if we would be certain of our own effectual calling. (1) The first is that of making some emotional feeling, or some particular crisis in our religious experience the basis of our assurance that we are effectually called. The Bible teaches us that men may have very strong feelings, and experiences, without being regenerated (Matt. 13:5, 20, 21; Heb. 6:4-8). Effectual calling *may* be sudden. But it may also be experienced in a gradual way. There may be strong feelings at a particular time that arise from the work of the Spirit in regeneration. But it is not always so. (2) The second danger is the temptation to excuse ourselves from our duty to accept the gospel because we have not been regenerated. People sometimes say that they would repent and believe if only they could. But they say that they cannot because God has not given them the Spirit. What they evidently believe is that they must first feel that they have the Spirit before they can have the duty to repent and believe. But this is not true. God calls all men to repent and believe. And it is the duty of all men to do it, without argument or delay. Furthermore, it is not given to any man to first know that he is regenerated, and then to repent and believe. It is only by obeying the gospel invitation that we can ever be sure that we have been regenerated by the Holy Spirit. It is only as we "give diligence to make our calling and election sure" (II Pet. 1:10) that we can be sure that we are effectually called of Christ.

Questions:

1. What two exceptions are there to the rule that "all men who are to be saved will be saved by the foolishness of preaching"?
2. Give Scripture proof that God saves men by gospel preaching.
3. Do all men who hear the gospel believe?
4. What is offered to those who hear the gospel? Is it offered to all?
5. What is wrong with saying that "salvation should be offered to the elect only"?
6. Is there some natural difference in men which makes some accept, and and others reject the gospel offer? Explain.
7. What is the invariable response of men to the gospel, while they are not regenerate?
8. What makes the gospel call effectual (in the case of some)?
9. What does Fig. A illustrate? What does Fig. B illustrate?
10. How does the raising of Lazarus illustrate effectual calling?
11. Does this doctrine make men "mere pawns on a chessboard"? Why?
12. What is the false idea of "irresistible grace"? What is the true idea?
13. Why is effectual calling "irresistible"? Give three items in your answer.
14. What are the two dangers to be avoided in being sure of our own case?

LESSON TWENTY-SIX

Question 86. What is faith in Jesus Christ?

Answer: Faith in Jesus Christ is a saving grace,[1] whereby we receive and rest upon him alone for salvation, as he is offered to us in the gospel.[2]

Question 87. What is repentance unto life?

Answer: Repentance unto life is a saving grace,[3] whereby a sinner, out of a true sense of his sin, and apprehension of the mercy of God in Christ,[4] doth, with grief and hatred of his sin, turn from it unto God,[5] with full purpose of, and endeavour after, new obedience.[6]

1. For by grace are ye saved through faith; and that not of yourselves, it is the gift of God (Eph. 2:8).

2. But as many as received him, to them gave he power to become the sons of God, even to them that believe on his name (John 1:12; cf. Gal. 2:16).

3. Then hath God also to the Gentiles granted repentance unto life (Acts 11:18).

4. Now when they heard this, they were pricked in their heart, and said . . . what shall we do? Then Peter said, . . . repent . . . (Acts 2:37, 38).

5. Then shall ye remember your own evil ways . . . and shall loathe yourselves in your own sight . . . (Ezek. 36:31).

6. For, behold . . . ye sorrowed after a godly sort . . . in all things ye have approved yourselves to be clear in this matter (II Cor. 7:11).

Effectual calling would not be what it is if it did not result in conversion. And since conversion always results from effectual calling, we depart at this point from the order of the Catechism. We consider the "second step" in the application of redemption.

But what is *conversion?* Conversion may be defined as a complete revolution in the mind (or heart, or soul) of man, whereby a sinner turns from all self-esteem and confidence to trust in Christ alone for salvation. We can perhaps see this in a clearer way if we illustrate:

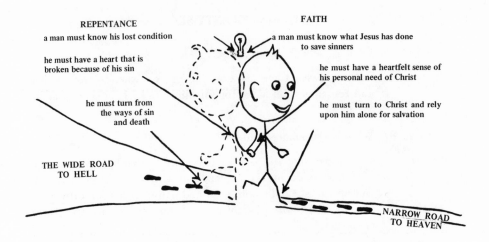

REPENTANCE
a man must know his lost condition

he must have a heart that is broken because of his sin

he must turn from the ways of sin and death

THE WIDE ROAD TO HELL

FAITH
a man must know what Jesus has done to save sinners

he must have a heartfelt sense of his personal need of Christ

he must turn to Christ and rely upon him alone for salvation

NARROW ROAD TO HEAVEN

Let us briefly consider the meaning of the illustration. (1) First, there is the entrance of *light* into the soul. The dead sinner (because he has first been regenerated by the Holy Spirit) is now able to receive the truth. He is able to understand the gospel. Jesus Christ, in other words, becomes a prophet to such a person. He teaches such a person by His Word and Spirit. And He teaches two things: the sinner's lost condition, and the sinner's need of Christ. The first element of true conversion, then, is correct knowledge of self and of Jesus Christ. (2) Secondly, there is the entrance of *heat* into the soul. We use this expression to indicate the fact that a regenerated person cannot receive the knowledge of the truth without also feeling a personal conviction of sin, and of the need of Christ as Savior. This does not mean that the element of feeling will necessarily be experienced "all at once," or that all true believers will experience this in the same way, or in the same degree. But no one can really be regenerated and then remain without sorrow of heart because of sin, and love toward Christ. (3) Then, thirdly, there is the entrance of *power* into the soul. When a man has come to see the truth as to his own need, and Christ's ability to answer that need—and when he has come to feel how urgent that need is, and how hopeless he is without Christ—

126

then it is that the gospel also demands action! The sinner must turn from sin, and turn to Christ in trust and dependence. It is only when a sinner has done this also, that we can say he is truly converted.

If we have grasped the significance of the above illustration, two things will be clear. First, it will be clear that conversion is the act of *man*. It is not God who repents and believes; it is the sinner. And it is just as important to stress this fact, as it is to stress the fact that it is God alone who effectually calls (or calls and regenerates) in the first place. It is for this reason that those who preach the gospel are to make it clear to all that they must be converted—that they must repent and believe—in order to be saved. Secondly, we note that because conversion follows effectual calling, in the order of the application of redemption, there is no place for any praise to the sinner. It is indeed the sinner who repents and believes. But *why* does he do so? It is only because God has given him a new nature (by regeneration) which can no longer resist the power of the gospel. How can a man resist what he knows to be true? How can he resist what he himself now desires? And how can he resist what he himself is determined to do? It is for this reason that the Bible can speak of faith and repentance not only as the activity of man, but also as the gift of God! So we read in Acts 11:18, "then hath God also to the Gentiles *granted* repentance unto life." And in Ephesians 2:8, we read, "by grace are ye saved through faith, and that not of yourselves; it is the *gift* of God"! It is our duty to repent and believe, in other words. But it is also our duty to give God the glory and praise because we have received from Him the new nature which made it possible for us to repent and believe.

From the above illustration we can also see the difference between true conversion (without which no man can be saved) and counterfeit conversion which is so common in our day. For example, a man may know the doctrines of the Christian faith "backwards and forwards," so to speak, and yet not be converted. Mere knowledge only makes us proud (I Cor. 8:1). When a man knows the true gospel, but feels no conviction of sin or love for Christ, and does not turn from a sin-dominated life to trust in and live for Him, he is not really converted. Again, a man may feel deep conviction of sin, and strong desire for salvation. But without true knowledge of the only way of salvation his feelings will profit him nothing. Or, to take yet another example, a man may decide to "turn over a new leaf." But if this is simply a "decision" of the human will, without knowledge and conviction of sin, it is not true conversion. True conversion, in other words, is something that affects the whole man, whereas "counterfeit conversion" affects only part of

127

man's nature. Because it affects only part of man's nature, it doesn't really result in any lasting change at all.

And this, in conclusion is something that we need to emphasize. Faith and repentance are not just sudden and momentary things. They are not something that we need for only a particular time in life. No, they are something that we must have throughout the Christian life. What we call conversion is really just the beginning of the activity of faith and repentance. When a man begins to truly repent and believe, we can say that he *is* converted. But he does not cease to repent and believe when (or because) he is converted. It is for this reason that we must be careful that we do not make the mistake of thinking that conversion is something that we can "look back on" in order to be sure that we are saved. Some denominations appear to teach that conversion is *always* the type of experience that a person can date on the calendar, and that one can therefore look back upon as a certain proof of salvation. The fact is, however, that conversion is often a very gradual experience (as in the case of Isaac, John the Baptist, and others; see Luke 1:15). There have been many true believers, in other words, who could not tell the precise time of conversion. And, according to the Bible, the only sure proof of conversion is not the suddenness of it, but the continuance of it, and the fruit that comes from it. If a person can truly say that he now lives, daily, the life of repentance and faith—and if there is in that person's life the evidence of the working of the Holy Spirit—there is no need to "worry" because the precise time of conversion cannot be recalled. The Bible does not say that we are to make our calling and election sure by looking back on a momentary experience. It rather says that we are to make our calling and election sure by "giving diligence" (II Pet. 1:10) and continuing in the way of faith, repentance, and obedience to the Lord.

Questions:

1. Why do we study questions 86 and 87 at this point rather than later on?
2. What is conversion?
3. What are the two essential "parts" of conversion?
4. What are the three necessary "elements" of conversion?
5. In your own words describe how the first element of conversion is taking place in Shorty.
6. In your own words describe how the second element is taking place.
7. In your own words describe how the third element is taking place.

8. Who is the only one who is active in conversion (repenting and believing)?
9. Why is it that the sinner can take no credit for repenting and believing?
10. What are some of the types of "counterfeit conversion"?
11. When does repentance and faith cease in the life of the Christian?
12. Is conversion always a momentary experience? Can it ever be?
13. Give an example of a conversion that could not have been "remembered" as having taken place on a certain date; and one that could be so "remembered."
14. How can we be sure that we have been converted?
15. How are we to seek assurance that we are elect and called of God?
16. Read the parable of Christ (Matt. 13:3-8, 18-23) and try to state what element (or elements) of true conversion were lacking in the first three cases mentioned by our Lord.

Question 32. What benefits do they that are effectually called partake of in this life?

Answer: They that are effectually called do in this life partake of justification,[1] adoption,[2] and sanctification, and the several benefits which in this life do either accompany or flow from them.[3]

Question 33. What is justification?

Answer: Justification is an act of God's free grace, wherein he pardoneth all our sins,[4] and accepteth us as righteous in his sight,[5] only for the righteousness of Christ imputed to us, and received by faith alone.[6]

1. . . . them he also justified (Rom. 8:30).

2. . . . unto the adoption . . . (Eph. 1:5).

3. . . . Christ Jesus, who of God is made unto us wisdom, and righteousness, and sanctification, and redemption (I Cor. 1:30).

4. In whom we have redemption through his blood, the forgiveness of sins, according to the riches of his grace (Eph. 1:7).

5. He hath made him to be sin for us, who knew no sin, that we might be made the righteousness of God in him (II Cor. 5:21).

6. . . . so by the obedience of one shall many be made righteous (Rom. 5:19). . . . a man is not justified by the works of the law, but by the faith of Jesus Christ, even we have believed . . . that we might be justified . . . (Gal. 2:16).

We have now considered (1) Effectual Calling and (2) Conversion. In this lesson we consider (3) Justification.

The great question that this doctrine answers is this: How can a guilty sinner be righteous before God? How can one who has sinned against God's perfect law thus becoming guilty, and subject to condemnation, be freed from this guilt and condemnation? What we need to think of, if we are to understand justification, is a guilty person standing before a just judge. "If there be controversy between men," says Moses, "and they come into judgment, that the judges may judge them; then they shall justify the righteous, and condemn the wicked" (Deut. 25:1). It can easily be seen, from this text, that when a judge justifies a man, he simply declares that man to be righteous. Likewise, when a judge condemns a man, he simply declares that he is wicked. This is very important. Justification is a declaration. It is God's judgment pronounced. It is His testimony that a particular person is not guilty in His sight, and therefore under no condemnation. But since all have sinned and come short of the glory of God (Rom. 3:23), the great difficulty is this: How can God declare a sinner to be righteous?

The answer to this is that God himself *makes* sinners righteous. Please note carefully that there is a difference between making sinners holy, and making sinners righteous. It is true, of course, that God not only makes sinners righteous (by justification), but that He also makes them holy (by sanctification). But the great glory of the gospel of Jesus Christ is that it freely offers to sinners a perfect righteousness which they may have even though they are *not* yet holy. And in order to illustrate how this is done, we will try to picture in a simple way the twofold imputation by which a sinner is made righteous before God. When we say *imputation* we mean that God has imputed (reckoned, regarded) to one person what originally belonged to another. For example, we speak of the imputation of Adam's sin. By this we mean that the sin of Adam—his guilt and condemnation—is "laid to the account" of all his posterity. In this imputation we receive something

from Adam, but he receives nothing from us. However, in the case of Jesus Christ and His elect people, there is a double imputation. (1) There is, first, the imputation of our guilt and condemnation to the Lord Jesus Christ. "For he [God] hath made him [Christ] to be sin for us," says the Apostle (II Cor. 5:21). Our sin was "laid to his account," and He was treated as if He had sinned our sin. (2) Then there is, secondly, the imputation of His righteousness to us. We are "made the righteousness of God in Him," says the Apostle (II Cor. 5:21). The perfect righteousness of Christ is "laid to our account." God treats us as if we had never sinned. He regards us as if we had kept all His holy laws perfectly.

It will be clearly seen, if the above illustration is understood, that *God* is the author of justification. "It is God that justifieth" (Rom. 8:33). It is God who makes us righteous. And it is God who declares that He has made us righteous. It is important to emphasize this, because many people misunderstand "justification by faith." Justification by faith does not mean that faith is something that makes us righteous. Faith is not a "good work" that pleases God in such a way that He considers it "just as good" as if we had obeyed His law perfectly. Faith is *not* the ground of our righteousness: the work of Jesus Christ alone is the ground of our righteousness. That is why faith, in order to save, must be a faith in Jesus Christ. Faith in any other will not save because there is no righteousness in any other. Neither is there in any other a sin-bearer on behalf of God's elect. *Faith is*, therefore, *an instrument only*. It is, as it were, "the hand by which we receive the righteousness of God." It is by faith that we receive the righteousness of God, but faith is not the source of that righteousness.

In order to see the glory of this justification more clearly, we need now to stress certain truths. One of these is the fact that a man can be justified only once. It is not possible for a man to be justified again and again. Justification is not a work (which is only gradually completed) but an act (which is completed in a moment). This is because of the fact that when Christ finished His life of obedience on earth He offered up to the Father for His elect people a perfect righteousness. And when He received the terrible punishment for their sins, He made a full payment for all of their sins. When a man repents of his sin and believes on the Lord Jesus Christ, in other words, he is from that moment onward—even through all eternity—legally righteous before God. He is no more subject to God's wrath and condemnation. "There is therefore now no condemnation to them which are in Christ Jesus" (Rom. 8:1). But another thing that we must stress is the fact that no man is justi-

132

fied until he repents and believes. Since Christ died for the ungodly many centuries ago, some have thought that God's elect people were already justified at that moment when Christ's work was finished. Others have supposed that they were justified from eternity because God had already planned to justify them before the world began. But the Bible clearly teaches us that this is not so. "You," says the Apostle, "*were* some time alienated, and enemies in your mind by wicked works, yet *now* hath he reconciled in the body of his flesh through death" (Col. 1:21, 22). And "we *have believed* in Jesus Christ," he says in another place, "that we *might be* justified" (Gal. 2:16). The reason for this is that there is a difference between God's plan and the execution of God's plan. There is a difference between what God has done to provide a basis for our justification, and what God does in making application of redemption to us.

In order to complete our discussion of justification, we need to consider briefly the relationship between faith and works. We know, says Paul, "that a man is not justified by the works of the law, but by the faith of Jesus Christ" (Gal. 2:16). What this means is that we are justified by faith alone. We do not neeed, in addition to repentance and faith, some measure of obedience to God's law in order to be justified. No matter how sinful a man has been, in other words, if he will only repent of his sin and believe in Christ, he will be justified immediately. He will "then and there" be righteous before God. Against this teaching it has always been said that this will encourage men to live in sin. But the Bible clearly teaches that when a man is truly repentant and believing—when a man is once justified, that is—*then* he will also begin to do "good works." These good works will be the "fruit of faith." They will come as a result of justification. It is for this reason that the Reformers always said that "we are justified by faith alone, but the faith that justifies is never alone." "For as the body without the spirit is dead, so faith without works is dead also" (James 2:26).

So important is this doctrine of justification by faith that it has been well called "the article of a standing or falling Church." If a Church teaches this doctrine faithfully, whatever faults and imperfections it may have, it is still worthy to be called a true Church of Christ. But if this doctrine is no longer maintained faithfully, it is no longer a Church of Christ Jesus. For here, perhaps more than in anything else, is seen the power and glory of the gospel.

Questions:

1. What is the great question that is answered by the doctrine of jus-

133

tification?
2. What does the Bible mean by the word "justify"? (Deut. 25:1).
3. What does the Bible mean by the word "condemn"?
4. Does justification mean that God makes sinners holy? Explain.
5. What is imputation?
6. Give another example of imputation other than that which involves Christ.
7. What are the two aspects of the imputation that involves Christ?
8. Explain how the picture illustrates this double imputation.
9. Who justifies the sinner?
10. What does justification by faith *not* mean?
11. How often can a man be justified? Why?
12. When is a man justified? Contrast the true view with two wrong views.
13. What is the relationship between faith and works?
14. How important is the doctrine of justification by faith?

(IMPORTANT MESSAGE)

FOR _____

DATE _____ TIME _____ A.M. / P.M.

M _____

OF _____

PHONE _____
AREA CODE   NUMBER   EXTENSION

TELEPHONED		PLEASE CALL	
CAME TO SEE YOU		WILL CALL AGAIN	
WANTS TO SEE YOU		RUSH	
RETURNED YOUR CALL		SPECIAL ATTENTION	

MESSAGE _____

_____

_____

_____

_____

_____

SIGNED _____

LITHO IN U.S.A.

TOPS FORM 3002P

LESSON TWENTY-EIGHT

Question 34. What is adoption?

Answer: Adoption is an act of God's free grace,[1] whereby we are received into the number, and have a right to all the privileges of the sons of God.[2]

1. Behold what manner of love the Father hath bestowed upon us, that we should be called the sons of God! (I John 3:1).

2. But as many as received him, to them gave he power to become the sons of God, even to them that believe on his name (John 1:12). And if children, then heirs; heirs of God, and joint-heirs with Christ: . . . that we may be glorified together (Rom. 8:17).

Adoption follows justification—not in *time,* necessarily, but—certainly in the *logical order* of things. This is obvious for the following reason: God cannot accept anyone into His family unless and until that one is made righteous before Him. There can never be a member of God's great family who is yet guilty in His sight. However, we should not think that adoption is consciously later in the experience of the believer. In the experience of the believer there can hardly be any sense of one (adoption) being later than the other (justification). For as soon as a man has repented and believed, he is then not only justified but also adopted as a son of God!

But what is adoption? Let us first observe that the biblical teaching has nothing in common with the popular teaching today which is called "the universal brotherhood of man." This doctrine, which is very prominent in the writings of modernist Protestants and Roman Catholics, is to the effect that all men are by nature (that is, because of a common origin) children of the same creator, and brothers the one to the other. Like most errors, of course, there is an element of truth in this. For it is indeed true that God "hath made of *one* blood all nations of men for to dwell on all the face of the earth" (Acts 17:26), and "we are also his [God's] offspring" because He created us all. For this reason the Christian is to consider every man on earth as a proper object of his loving concern (Luke 10:29f.; Matt. 5:

135

44, 45). The Scripture even speaks of God as the Father of spirits (Heb. 12:9). But in spite of this element of the teaching of Scripture, it is not proper to speak of "the universal fatherhood of God and the universal brotherhood of man." This is because of the fact that the whole human race sinned in Adam and fell with him in his first transgression. When this happened, men were alienated from God. They ceased to be "children" in the true sense of the word. Instead they became children of the devil. When Jesus said to the unbelieving people, "ye are of your father the devil" (John 8:44), He made it perfectly clear that sinful men are not the children of God, by nature.

It is this which leads us to understand why the Bible teaches that only some men are the children of God, and that they become the children of God only by adoption. If we are to think of sinful men and their relationship with God in the correct way, then we must see that they are more like homeless orphans than happy members of God's great family. They are the children of Satan, but Satan does not love them. And they do not belong to a family in which there is love the one for the other as among brothers and sisters. Just as many children in orphanages are there because their fathers and mothers do not love them, and do not want to take care of them, so sinful men are "aliens from the commonwealth of Israel, and strangers from the covenants of promise, having no hope, and without God in the world" (Eph. 2:12). Let us illustrate:

When a person is adopted, he becomes a member of the redeemed family of God. Adoption is the act of God, by which a person (who has been regenerated, converted, and justified) is transferred from the lost human race into the fellowship of the redeemed. This change is just as vivid and dramatic as that which is pictured in our illustration. Here we see homeless Shorty suddenly taken into a new relationship. He now has someone who cares for him. He will never again be forsaken. For, as the Bible says, "God sent forth his Son . . . to redeem them that were under the law, that we might receive the adoption of sons, and because ye are sons, God hath sent forth the Spirit of his Son into your hearts, crying, Abba, Father. Wherefore thou art no more a servant, but a son" (Gal. 4:4-6).

There are several things that we must emphasize if we are to fully appreciate the wonder of adoption. (1) Adoption is something that takes effect in a moment of time. It is an *act* of God: something that is done all at once. It is not a *work* of God which takes a long period of time. (2) Adoption is also something that remains in effect permanently. Those whom the Father adopts will never again be forsaken. No one, says Jesus, "is able to pluck them out of my Father's hand" (John 10:29). When we become the children of God by adoption, we are in the Father's hand. And no one—not even Satan—can ever take us out of His hand again. (3) Adoption is also something of which we are made conscious. For "because ye are sons," says the Bible, "God hath sent forth the Spirit of his Son into your hearts, crying, Abba, Father" (Gal. 4:6). And "the Spirit itself beareth witness with our spirit, that we are the children of God" (Rom. 8:16). God not only makes us His sons, in other words, but He also makes us aware of the fact that we are His sons.

But *how*, it may be asked, does God make us aware of the fact that we are are His sons? What does it mean when the Bible says that "the Spirit itself beareth witness with our spirits that we are the children of God"? In answer to this, let us observe: (1) first, that the witness (testimony) by which we know this is a joint witness. It is not our own spirit (or heart, or mind) which says this, without the Holy Spirit. And neither is it the Holy Spirit that says this, without our spirit. It is only when the two "speak" the same thing at the same time that we have this joint witness of which the Bible speaks. (2) In the second place, we must remember that the Scripture is the Spirit's testimony. "To the law and to the testimony," says the prophet, "if they speak not according to this word, it is because there is no light in them" (Isa. 8:20). We can never be sure that it really is the Spirit of God (rather than some evil spirit) which is speaking to us, unless it is according to the Scriptures. (3) This leads us to say, in the third place, that the witness of the Spirit with our spirits can be experienced only when God enables us to say of ourselves what Scripture says about true believers. For example: the Bible says that whosoever believes on Jesus Christ shall not perish, but have eternal life. If God enables me to say, sincerely, "I believe in Jesus Christ," then I have this joint witness by which I can know that I belong to Him. For in this case I say of myself what the Spirit (in Scripture) likewise says of true believers.

In our thinking on the subject of adoption there is an important difference that we must always keep in mind. This is the difference between our sonship and that of Jesus Christ. For He is the only begotten Son of God (John 1:18, etc.). Our Lord Jesus Christ is the same in substance with the Father, and equal in power and glory, as respects His divine nature. And this means that He is God. We must always remember that when we become the sons of God by adoption this does not make us "divine." We do not share with Christ in this equality with the Father. We are—and ever shall be—nothing more than creatures of God. And we must be on our guard against those who speak of adoption as if it made us just like Jesus Christ in every respect.

But we may well ask: Does this in any way decrease the wonder of our adoption? And the answer must be: No, not at all! Rather does it increase the wonder of it. For when we are adopted, we (who are mere creatures) are yet brought to share in the things that belong by birthright only to our Lord. We as "children" become "heirs of God, and joint-heirs with Christ" (Gal. 4:17). He becomes our elder brother, and great are the benefits which God, for His sake, grants unto us. Even now we are completely delivered from the bondage of fear, because we are accepted in Christ (Rom. 8:15). We are led by the Holy Spirit in pathways of truth and righteousness (8:14). We are enabled to come boldly to the throne of grace in prayer (Heb. 4:16) to find help in the time of need. We have God's unfailing care in all that befalls us (Ps. 103:13; 125; Rom. 8:29-35; etc.). And even though we are subject to His corrective discipline, it is only in love that the Father chastens us (Heb. 12:6-11). And best of all, our Father promises that He will never leave or forsake us (Lam. 3:31, 32), because He has sealed us unto the day of redemption by the Holy Spirit of Christ (Eph. 4:30). So it is not possible that those who have been adopted shall fail of the grace of God (I Pet. 1:3, 4). And while "it doth not yet appear what we shall be . . . we know that, when he shall appear, we shall be like him, for we shall see him as he is" (I John 3:2).

138

Questions:

1. Why must adoption logically follow justification?
2. Why do we say "logically" rather than "chronologically" in Question 1 above?
3. What is the modernist error as respects the matter of sonship with God?
4. What is the element of truth in this? What is the error? Prove.
5. With what are men (in their natural born sinful state) compared in the illustration? With what are the saved persons compared?
6. How long does adoption take? How long does it remain in effect?
7. Are we conscious of our adoption? Prove.
8. How does the Spirit bear witness with our spirits?
9. What is the difference between our sonship and that of Christ?
10. Does this difference decrease the wonder of our sonship? Why?
11. What are some of the blessings belonging to our sonship?
12. When will we enjoy the complete benefit of adoption? Prove.

LESSON TWENTY-NINE

Question 35. What is sanctification?

Answer:　　Sanctification is the work of God's free grace,[1] whereby we are renewed in the whole man after the image of God,[2] and are enabled more and more to die unto sin, and live unto righteousness.[3]

1. God hath from the beginning chosen you to salvation, through sanctification of the Spirit (II Thess. 2:13).

2. And be renewed in the spirit of your mind . . . that ye put on the new man, which after God is created in righteousness and true holiness (Eph. 4:23, 24).

3. As Christ was raised up from the dead . . . even so we also should walk in newness of life . . . henceforth we should not serve sin (Rom. 6:4, 6).

Sanctification, which follows upon justification and adoption in the order of salvation, is also of God's free grace. It is not merited by any man. It is not anything for which a sanctified man can take any credit. For it is not man who sanctifies himself but God only. As we shall see, however, it is accomplished in such a way that man himself is active and responsible in the process of sanctification. The Bible commands us to "work out [our] own salvation with fear and trembling" but it is only "because it is God which worketh in [us] both to will and to do of his good pleasure" (Phil. 2:12, 13). It is this which presents us with the problem: How can sanctification be the work of God, and yet (at the same time) a work of man?

In answer to this question we may stress three points. (1) First, the work of *sanctification begins with an inward change.* And this inward change is the work of God. It is called regeneration. "Ye have put off the old man with his deeds," says the Apostle, "and have put on the new man, which is renewed in knowledge after the image of him that created him" (Col. 3:10). What we must see, however, is this: while the whole nature of man is renewed by regeneration, it is not made perfect or complete in that one momentary act.

140

There are several ways in which we might try to illustrate this truth. For example: a baby is a "new creature," but it has a long way to go before it becomes a full grown human person. Or again: when a man has a terrible disease, and is given one of the new "wonder" drugs, he will suddenly be delivered from the power of that disease. But he will still have a long way to go before he is completely strong and well.

In much the same way, when a man is regenerated, he passes from death unto life—he is no longer under the dominion of sin—and yet the power of sin is not yet entirely gone. The effects of the disease (original sin) are still there. And sanctification is the work of the Holy Spirit by which the "new nature" more and more gets the victory over this remaining power of indwelling sin.

(2) We see, then, that *the work of sanctification is also gradual.* It is not something that is done all at once (like justification, or adoption). It is a work rather than an act. It is never entirely completed in anyone in this present life. But this brings us to look more closely at the human side of the matter. Because this work is going on, in the heart of the believer, it necessarily follows that there will be (in his experience) a constant conflict with sin. As John said, "every man that hath this hope in him purifieth himself, even as he [the Lord] is pure" (I John 3:3). A regenerated man cannot live in peace with sin (I John 3:6-9). This is not possible because "whosoever is born of God doth not commit [or practice] sin; for his [God's] seed remaineth

141

in him: and he cannot sin, because he is born of God" (I John 3:9). When a man's heart has been changed—and as it is further conformed to the image of Christ—it is not possible for sin to have the dominion. Yes, the believer will sin. But he will never say, "It is all right." He will never want to sin. He will never be satisfied with himself. No, he will always be fighting with himself because he hates his own sin! It is in this light only that we can explain what Paul says in Romans 7:7-25. Does Paul say that he sins? Yes. He does what he does not want to do, and he does not do what he wants to do, often. But does he feel satisfied with this? No. He says he is "wretched." And he says he is warring against sin right in his own mind. But the wonderful thing is that he also knows that he will have the victory through the Lord Jesus Christ. It is a slow process, to be sure, but it is also certain.

(3) Finally we note that *the work of sanctification is synergistic.* Synergistic means a work in which man cooperates with God. It is a work in which both man and God are active. This does not mean that the work of man is equal with the work of God. It is not. The work of God is such that God gets all the credit for man's sanctification. And the work of man is such that he is never anything more than an "unprofitable servant." But the important point is that there is no such thing as sanctification except where God and man are both working—God is working in us to will and to do of His good pleasure, and we are working out our own salvation with fear and trembling (Phil. 2:12, 13). We must purify ourselves. But we must also remember that it is God alone who enables us to do it!

We see, then, that there is one sure evidence of sanctification. Only the man who is more and more dying to sin, and more and more living unto righteousness, is really being sanctified. "We know," says John, "that everyone that doeth righteousness is born of him" (I John 2:29). "For this is the love of God, that we keep his commandments: and his commandments are not grievous" (5:3). This does not mean that the true believer keeps the law of God perfectly. No man can say that he does that (I John 1:8, 10). Yet the true believer does strive to do it. He loves the law of God. It does not grieve him. And more and more he does keep it, though yet imperfectly. It is for this reason that the Scripture says that "faith without works is dead" (James 2:20). The unbeliever, to be sure, may do certain things that seem to be good works. They may even be, in the eyes of other men, the same things that believers do—such as putting money in the offering at Church. Yet there is really a world of difference. (1) The true believer is glad that God requires the high and holy things that He requires, whereas the unbeliever is not. (2) The true believer does what he does out of gratitude. He says, "God has already saved me, so now I want to please Him." But the unbeliever is always "trying to do good" so as to gain God's favor, or to prove his own goodness. (3) Again, the true believer will realize that even in his "best" works, he does not begin to "measure up" to what he ought to be and do. The unbeliever does not realize this, but is satisfied with what he is, and has done.

This brings us to observe, in conclusion, that *humility* is the great virtue that we find in those who are being sanctified. This is something that we notice again and again in the lives of God's great servants, as we learn of them in the Bible. As we study the lives of such men as Moses, David, Peter, Paul, and so on, we see how they fought against sin within themselves. We see how they sometimes fell back. But then we see how they always went back to fight against sin more than ever before. Then we notice two things: on the one hand we see that they are becoming more holy in their lives, and on the other hand we see that they are coming to feel more and more their own unworthiness before God. Or, in other words, the more they come to be holy, the more they feel themselves to be sinners! And while this may seem very strange at first thought, it is not really difficult to understand. Let us illustrate. Imagine a man who has fallen into the mud on a dark night. Now at a distance he sees a great light. He also begins to see how dirty he is. And he begins to wash off the dirt as he walks toward the light. So the nearer he gets to the light, the more dirt he tries to get rid of. And yet, because he is getting nearer to the light, it is also true that he is able to see more clearly how dirty he is. So it is with those who are being sanctified by the Spirit. The Holy Spirit is constantly showing them more and more of the Lord Jesus Christ. The Holy Spirit is constantly showing them how high and holy is the law of God. And the Holy Spirit is constantly leading them to cleanse themselves of their old sins. They are becoming less sinful. Yet because they are seeing more and more clearly what thy ought to be, they also feel more and more that they are unworthy sinners. This is the reason why the holiest men (in Bible history and in Church history) were also the humblest men. Others could see that they were indeed dying more and more unto sin, and living unto righteousness. But at the same time, they could see more and more that they were sinners saved by grace!

We might sum it all up, then, by saying that sanctification is not a process by which we go higher and higher, until we can stand before God feeling that we are holy people. It is rather a process by which we go lower and lower in our estimate of self, while at the same time we desire above all that we might be holy. For it is only in genuine humility that we really become holy!

Questions:

1. Who should have the credit for man's sanctification? Why?
2. How does God sanctify us?
3. When does God sanctify us?
4. Where does God sanctify us?
5. Of what is sanctification a continuation?
6. In your own words tell how the illustration shows what sanctification is.
7. How long does sanctification take?
8. What do we mean when we say that sanctification is "synergistic"?
9. What is the sure evidence of sanctification?
10. What are some of the differences between the works of true believer and unbelievers?
11. What is the great virtue that we find in those who are being sanctified?
12. Why is this so?
13. Does the true believer feel that he is becoming holy? Explain.

LESSON THIRTY

Question 36. What are the benefits which in this life do accompany or flow from justification, adoption, and sanctification?

Answer: The benefits which in this life do accompany or flow from justification, adoption, and sanctification, are, assurance of God's love, peace of conscience, joy in the Holy Ghost,[1] increase of grace,[2] and perseverance therein to the end.[3]

1. Being justified by faith, we have peace with God . . . and rejoice in hope of the glory of God . . . and hope maketh not ashamed, because the love of God is shed abroad in our hearts by the Holy Ghost, which is given unto us (Rom. 5:1, 2, 5).
2. The path of the just is as the shining light, that shineth more and more unto the perfect day (Prov. 4:18).
3. Wherefore . . . brethren, give diligence to make your calling and election sure: for if ye do these things, ye shall never fall (II Pet. 1:10).

Justification, adoption, and sanctification are not the only benefits of grace. Why then does the Catechism devote more attention to justification, adoption, and sanctification than it does to these other benefits? The answer is: (1) because justification, adoption, and sanctification are absolutely necessary to salvation. No one can be saved without these benefits. All believers *are* justified and adopted. And all are being sanctified. But we cannot always say that all believers enjoy the other benefits of grace. (2) This is because the other benefits (such as assurance, peace, joy, etc.) either accompany or flow from justification, adoption, and sanctification. They do not stand by themselves, in other words, but are in a certain sense dependent upon the "chief benefits." Take, for example, assurance of God's love. Now the fact is that true believers do not all—and do not at all times—have this benefit of redemption. There are at least two cases in which this is obvious. A recently converted sinner may not yet realize that he can know that he is one of God's elect. He may not know the Bible sufficiently to know this. No doubt this is why there are texts in the Bible which encourge such persons to

145

get that assurance. "Give diligence," says Peter (II Pet. 1:10), "to make your calling and election sure, for if ye do these things, ye shall never fall." John (I John 5:13) likewise writes to tell us that we can make sure that we have eternal life. So we see that a believer does not necessarily obtain assurance as soon as he believes, at least not "the full assurance" of which the Bible speaks (Heb. 6:11). Another case is that of the man who has had assurance, and then (because of some such evil as that which befell Peter or David) comes to doubt of his own standing with God (see Ps. 51:8, 12; Ps. 77, etc.). There are many expressions of this lack of assurance in the Psalms. But because God never forsakes those who are regenerated, converted, justified, and adopted, those who lose their assurance for a time may also regain it. This they ought to do. And this they may do again by giving diligence to make their calling and election sure. Here we see again the important relationship between God's work of grace in the believer, and the responsibility of the believer. *God* never forsakes any true believer, not even when he temporarily fails to do what he ought to do. But this does not change the fact that until *he* (the erring believer) mends his ways again, and returns to diligence, he will not have the assurance that he belongs to God.

Another benefit that is closely related to assurance is peace of conscience. So is joy in the Holy Ghost. This can be seen from the fact that Paul sometimes appealed to the testimony of his own conscience, and to his inward sense of joy, in proof of the fact that he possessed assurance of God's love (II Cor. 1:12; II Tim. 1:3, etc.). The conscience of the believer is at peace because the believer has put his trust in the sacrifice of Jesus Christ, and is seeking to do those things that are pleasing to God as an expression of gratitude to Christ. It is this too which gives the believer joy. For what greater joy could there be than to know that the Lord Jesus Christ has paid the penalty for sin? So it is hard to think of one of these benefits without thinking of others. When the believer is diligent and faithful, in other words, then these benefits will all be given in richer measure. And if he is not diligent, then all will in some measure be lost for a time. When David fell into grievous sin, for example, he didn't merely lose assurance, but also peace of conscience and joy in the Holy Ghost. That is why he prayed, "restore unto me the joy of thy salvation" when he also prayed "cast me not away" (Ps. 51:10, 11).

One of the great conflicts in the history of the Church has come to focus at this point: *Can a true believer fall?* In answer to this question we shall have to say, *yes*, a true believer can fall in his diligence and faithfulness to

God, but we shall have to say, *no,* a true believer can never fall out of God's mercy and grace, which are unto everlasting life. This may be illustrated (as C. H. Spurgeon once said) by a man on board a great ship. If he is not careful he may indeed fall down on board that ship, and injure himself. But so great and so safe is the ship that he will never fall overboard. This may not be literally true of any ship. But it is true of God's grace. Christ said, of all true believers, "I give unto them eternal life; and they shall never perish, neither shall any[one] pluck them out of my hand" (John 10:28). It is for this reason that there will always be "increase of grace, and perseverance therein to the end" in the life of every true beliver.

We have tried to illustrate the doctrine of perseverance in a simple way. Shorty has been given the training and encouragement that he needs to run a good race. The coach knows that he will make it all right. But this does not mean that it will be easy! It does not mean that Shorty will win first prize even if he is careless and only half-hearted. No, he will have to make an effort. He will have to run as hard as he can. And it will not be easy.

The doctrine of perseverance, in other words, does not mean certain things that people have sometimes imagined. (1) It does not mean that all members of the *visible* Church will be saved. It does not mean that all who are "covenant born, baptized, or instructed" will persevere. We know this because there have been some (such as Judas) who were members of the Church and yet did not persevere. John speaks of such people when he says, "they went out from us, but they were not of us; for if they had been of us, they would no doubt have continued with us, but they went out, that they might be made manifest that they were not all of us" (I John 2:19). Here we see that people do appear to fall "out of" grace. But as John shows us that this is not really what has happened, we see that what really happened is that they only appeared to be in grace (true believers) to begin with. (2) Another thing that perseverance does not mean is that true believers will be saved "no matter what they do." When people imagine that this is what perseverance means, they only show that they do not understand. For, as the Catechism says, perseverance flows from justification, adoption, and sanctification. In other

147

words, it never belongs to anyone unless he is converted in his heart, and unless the Holy Spirit dwells in him. And it just is not possible for a man who has been changed in heart to go on living in sin just as before. It is not possible for a man in whom the Holy Spirit dwells, to live at peace with sin. No, in the nature of the case, he is going to want to fight against sin. So even though he may at times slip back, he will never be content until he returns to the battle against sin. (3) And finally we note that perseverance does not mean that true believers are saved by their own effort. It is quite true, of course, that perseverance takes effort. It is quite true that the believer *must* give diligence to make his calling and election sure. No one will be saved who does not make the effort to become holy. But the Bible is perfectly clear: it is God who works in us to will and do of his good pleasure; it is God who must have the entire praise when we persevere in grace. John expresses this quite clearly when he says, "whosoever is born of God doth not commit sin; for his [God's] seed remaineth in him: and he cannot sin, because he is born of God" (I John 3:9). The sin referred to in this verse is probably "the sin unto death" (see I John 5:16). The "sin unto death" is no doubt the sin that we see in those who profess faith in Christ, and then turn away from Christ again. This a true believer will never do. This a true believer can never do. And he can never do it because "he is begotten of God" and "keepeth himself" so that the "wicked one toucheth him not" (I John 5:18). And it is clearly God who alone must receive the credit since it is God who has given the believer the grace—the new nature and the will and power—to keep him ever persevering.

Perhaps the most important thing to emphasize in our view of the benefits that flow from justification, adoption, and sanctification, is this: these benefits do not come to the believer in any "automatic" way. He must "give diligence to make his calling and election sure" (II Pet. 1:10). He must seek these things in order to find them. But again we hasten to add: every true believer *will* find them in due time and measure, because of God's work of grace in his heart. So we must never forget to say, "thanks be to God, which giveth us the victory through our Lord Jesus Christ" (I Cor. 15:57).

Questions:

1. Why does the Catechism devote more attention to justification, adoption, and sanctification, than to the several benefits which flow from these?
2. Does every true believer have "assurance of God's love"? Explain.
3. May every true believer have "assurance"? Prove.

4. Can those who have it lose it? Explain.
5. From what does peace of conscience come?
6. Can one have "joy in the Holy Ghost" without assurance and peace?
7. Can a true believer fall? Explain.
8. How does the picture illustrate perseverance?
9. Does perseverance mean that all Church members will be saved? Why? Prove.
10. Why is it false to say that believers will be saved no matter what they do?
11. Who gets the credit for the perseverance of the believer? Why?
12. What is "the sin unto death"? Why must we reject the idea of "automatic"?

LESSON THIRTY-ONE

Question 37. What benefits do believers receive from Christ at death?

Answer: The souls of believers are at their death made perfect in holiness,[1] and do immediately pass into glory;[2] and their bodies, being still united to Christ,[3] do rest in their graves till the resurrection.[4]

1. . . . the spirits of just men made perfect (Heb. 12:23).

2. And Jesus said unto him, verily I say unto thee, today shalt thou be with me in paradise (Luke 23:43).

3. . . . them also which sleep in Jesus (I Thess. 4:14).

4. . . . they shall rest in their beds . . . (Isa. 57:2). . . . The hour is coming, in the which all that are in the graves shall hear his voice, and shall come forth . . . (John 5:28, 29).

We here consider what has been called "the intermediate state." Man does *not* reach his final state when he dies. But neither does he remain in the same state that he was in before the time of death. It is therefore intermediate. It stands between man's present state, and his final state.

To understand the intermediate state we need to remember that when God created man, He made him dichotomous (see Lesson 8). There are two aspects to human nature, then, the body and the soul (or, spirit). And death is simply a name for that event by which the soul (or, spirit) and body are separated the one from the other. Thus, when man dies, the body returns to the dust (Gen. 3:9; Acts 13:36) and sees corruption. This is true whether or not a man is a believer. As respects the physical body, in other words, we can see no difference in what happens to the believer at death, and what happens to the unbeliever. And yet, the Bible tells us that there is a great difference. Believers' souls are then made holy, and do immediately pass into glory (Luke 23:43; Rev. 14:13; Luke 16:19-31), whereas the souls of unbelievers begin at once to experience the torments of hell. So we could say, in other words, that the intermediate state is the same for believers and

150

unbelievers so far as the body is concerned, and entirely different so far as the soul or spirit is concerned. (Although, of course, even in death the physical body of the unbeliever belongs to the Lord, and is preserved for the resurrection unto life everlasting. And the body of the unbeliever belongs not to Him, but is reserved only to the resurrection of damnation.) We illustrate the intermediate state (for the believer) below. It is understood, of course, that the soul or spirit is really invisible, and not a "ghost shaped like a body."

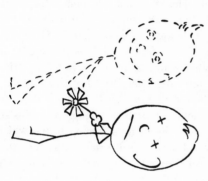

With this teaching of Scripture firmly in mind, we can firmly reject the doctrine of some of the modern cults. It is the doctrine of "soul sleep," which teaches that there is no conscious state of existence for the soul after death, prior to the resurrection. Now it is indeed true that the Bible speaks of the death of believers (but *not* unbelievers) as a "sleep," but this is because of the fact that there is a striking similarity between sleep and the death of the believer. (1) For one thing, there is the obvious fact that the body in death looks very similar to the body asleep. A sleeping person may appear dead, and a dead person appear as only asleep. (2) Then there is also the fact that a dead person is no longer conscious of events going on in the world. This is also true when a person is sleeping. (3) Then there is also the fact that there is a consciousness of the soul even during sleep, as is evident from the fact that sleeping persons dream. And so it is with those who die in the Lord. There is a conscious activity of the soul or spirit after death. For such reasons as these, we do not believe that there is such a thing as "soul sleep," by which certain cults mean *a state of darkness and unconsciousness* in which even believers "know nothing."

We must also reject, as equally unscriptural, the Roman Catholic dogma of purgatory. According to the teaching of Rome, when an ordinary believer dies (that is, all but a very few exceptionally holy saints) he must go to an intermediate *place*. This is not heaven, and it is not hell. It is rather a place where believers are said to suffer the temporal punishment for their sins until they have purified themselves. Some may remain there a very long time.

Others may remain only a short time. Meanwhile, the prayers of others, and merits of others, and the "offerings" of the mass by those who are still "on earth" can help to shorten that suffering. This teaching is completely contrary to the Bible. It can never be believed by those who know that Christ himself suffered alone the full penalty for all the sins of His people. The believer knows that He has perfected forever them that are sanctified by the one offering which He offered unto God. And so it is not surprising that Scripture nowhere teaches any such thing as this doctrine of purgatory.

We live in a day in which the *body* is often greatly undervalued as far as salvation and eternal life are concerned. Thus it is not uncommon for Christian people to talk as if the soul was all that mattered, and as if the body had no part in the saving program of God. It is for this reason that the Catechism reminds us that even in death the body is not forgotten. It is still united to Christ (in the case of believers). In other words, it is not forgotten by Him, as if only the soul mattered. For, as Job said (Job 19:26), "after my skin worms destroy this body, yet in my flesh shall I see God: whom I shall see for myself, and mine eyes shall behold, and not another: though my reins be consumed within me." For, as Jesus said, "the hour is coming in the which all that are in the graves shall hear his voice, and shall come forth; they that have done good, unto the resurrection of life; and they that have done evil, unto the resurrection of damnation" (John 5:28, 29). So it is the body which sleeps: but only until that great day. And we must be careful that we do not come to think of this intermediate state as if it were the final and complete hope of the believer! In Paul's second epistle to the Corinthians (5:1-8), he speaks of the intermediate state as falling short of his ultimate hope. It is like being "unclothed," or "undressed." And while Paul was willing to be absent from the body and present with the Lord, in this intermediate state, his great desire was to be "clothed upon, that mortality might be swallowed up of life" in resurrection (v. 4). So the great longing of the believer is not for the intermediate state as such, but only for the intermediate state *as a step toward* the great final state. So "we ourselves groan within ourselves, waiting for the adoption, to wit, the resurrection of our body" (Rom. 8:23).

One question has often been asked, in connection with death. Since death is "the wages of sin," why are believers required to die (since all their sins are already forgiven)? The Larger Catechism reminds us of several things that are helpful. (1) For one thing, death itself will one day lose *all* power over the believer. Death will then be "destroyed" (I Cor. 15:26). And believers will be delivered from it forever (v. 54). (2) But even now, says the Bible,

152

death has lost its sting so far as believers are concerned. If a man belongs to Christ, in other words, then death cannot hurt him (vv. 55, 56). (3) And even though it is still an enemy, a terror from which we shrink, the Bible assures us that God will use it for good. Like all other "evils" that believers are required to experience, death too is a means of sanctification. (4) But there is yet a better way, perhaps, of expressing the answer to our question. According to the Bible man *is* by nature dead in trespasses and sins (Eph. 2:1). As God said to Adam, "in the day that thou eatest thereof thou shalt surely die," so when one man sinned, death passed upon all men (Gen. 2:17; Rom. 5:12). We must not think, then, that death is something that just begins after a man stops breathing. Rather is death something that began when man sinned, and it comes to full manifestation only when both body and soul together are cast into the pit of God's wrath and destruction. But God in His mercy has retarded—or slowed down—the process by which this end is reached. And then, out of death He takes some men by His saving grace. It is for this reason that the regeneration of the soul is often called a passing from death unto life (I John 3:14). God *now* delivers our souls from the power of death, and at the last day He will likewise deliver our bodies from that power (John 5:25-29). God does not *yet* deliver the bodies of believers from the power of death in order that the saved and the lost might continue to live together in this world. Only in this way can the work of God's kingdom go on (as in the preaching of the gospel to the lost). So we are not yet delivered from the power of death as to the body, as we are in soul or spirit, in order that we might serve God's purpose in this world. Only when He has called out all of His elect will physical death itself be abolished.

Questions:

1. What is meant by "the intermediate state"?
2. What is death?
3. In what respect is the death of believer and unbeliever "the same"?
4. In what respect is it not the same?
5. What happens to the soul of the believer at death? Prove.
6. What is the doctrine of "soul sleep"? Give Scripture proof against.
7. Does the Bible use the word "sleep" as a description of those who are dead? Why?
8. What does the Roman Catholic Church teach as concerns believers at death?
9. Prove this Roman Catholic teaching to be wrong.

10. Is it right to emphasize the salvation of the soul more than the salvation of the body? Why?
11. Did Paul look forward to the "intermediate state"? Explain (from II Cor. 5:1-8).
12. What are some of the things that enable us to feel that death is not the terrible thing for the Christian that it is for the unbeliever?
13. Why doesn't God deliver us from death immediately?
14. If death is commonly meant as the separation of body and soul, is there a broader use of the word "dead" in Scripture? Explain.

LESSON THIRTY-TWO

Question 38. What benefits do believers receive from Christ at the resurrection?

Answer: At the resurrection, believers being raised up in glory,[1] shall be openly acknowledged and acquitted in the day of judgment,[2] and made perfectly blessed in the full enjoying of God[3] to all eternity.[4]

1. . . . all that are in the graves shall hear his voice, and shall come forth; they that have done good, unto the resurrection of life . . . (John 5:28, 29).

2. Whosoever therefore shall confess me before men, him will I confess before my Father which is in heaven (Matt. 10:32). Well done, good and faithful servant . . . enter thou into the joy of thy Lord (Matt. 25:23).

3. . . . we know that, when he shall appear, we shall be like him, for we shall see him as he is (I John 3:2). For now we see through a glass, darkly; but then face to face (I Cor. 13:12).

4. . . . so shall we ever be with the Lord (I Thess. 4:17).

The doctrine of the resurrection of the *body* has always been at the heart of the Christian faith. But it has also been a great offense to the unconverted heart of man. The "wise" Athenians listened politely to Paul for a time, but "when they heard of the resurrection of the dead, some mocked: and others said, We will hear thee again of this matter" (Acts 26:8). The Apostle believed that God would raise the dead bodies of men to life again. And "if there be no resurrection of the dead," he said, "then is Christ not risen," and the whole Christian faith is a vain and worthless thing (I Cor. 15:13ff.).

But what is meant by *resurrection*? It is simply this: the physical body which is laid in the grave and rots away, will one day rise again to stand upon the earth. The word "resurrection" means, literally, to stand up again. It is sometimes said today that things have now come to pass in our modern age which make it impossible to believe this doctrine any more. And what are these things that have happened? Well, some human bodies have been completely dissolved in the terrible fire of an atomic bomb. Not a trace of them can be found. And now, we are told, science has shown that the substance of a dead body decomposes and becomes a sort of "fertilizer" for other life. So it is said that a dead body may "become" the substance of a plant, and then an animal may eat the plant, and then a man may eat the animal, and so on. (We know, of course, that there have even been cannibals who have eaten other men.) So it just isn't "reasonable," we are told, to believe this doctrine of the resurrection of the body.

In answer to such unbelieving arguments let us first understand that writers of the Bible were not ignorant of these "problems." They knew about people who had felt "the violence of fire" (Heb. 11:34). They knew about "cannibalism" (Deut. 28:53). And yet they believed in the resurrection of the body. And there is one very good reason. They believed it because they saw the Lord Jesus Christ risen from the grave. They saw the scars made by the nails in His hands and feet. And so they believed that God could, and would, raise the dead on the last day as He has promised. They believed this even though they could not explain—or understand—*how* it could be. Paul, for example, never claimed to be able to explain *how* God would do this, but he does insist *that* God will do it. And his great argument is simply the fact that God is God. There is, in other words, no escape from this: we cannot really be Christians unless we are willing to believe in a "wonder-working God"—a God who is able to do far more than we can ask or even think. As Jesus said, "with men this is impossible, but with God all things are possible" (Matt. 19:26).

However, in I Corinthians 15 the Apostle gives us some assistance. He compares the body which is laid in the grave (to rot away) with a grain of wheat, or some other grain (I Cor. 15:37). The grain of wheat dies. It rots in the ground. And yet it also produces new life. Out of it comes a plant of the same identity as the grain. A grain of wheat, when planted, never produces anything but wheat. So we are to understand that when the body rots in the grave, everything that shows the evidence of sin in this present physical body will die forever. And yet, out of the body which is buried will come the body which rises again. Perhaps another illustration will help. An old Model-T Ford can be cast into the junk heap, and melted down into steel. Then the steel, purified of dross, can be used to make a new and up-to-date model. We can then say: this is the same car (in substance) and yet how different (in quality). Or, let us take yet another illustration. When an infant is in its mother's womb, as yet unborn, it is not very much like it will be as a full-grown adult. Yet who can deny that it is the same? The essential points to keep in mind—and in faith—then, are these: (1) the resurrection body will be the same body, as to substance and identity, but (2) it will be different as to its qualities and powers. God will *not* make us a new body out of nothing. He will not make us a similar body out of something else. But He will make us a *renewed* body out of the old. He will do it by raising up the old so that it will put on incorruption and immortality.

When the last day comes, the Bible says that Christ will return to the world. At that time all men without exception will be raised from the grave (John 5:28ff.). There will be an instantaneous perfecting of the bodies of believers, so that they will be like Christ in body as well as soul (I John 3:2). The world itself will, at that day, burn with an awesome fire out of which will come new heavens and a new earth (II Pet. 3:11ff.). The whole human race will then be assembled before the judgment seat of Christ, that everyone may give account of the things he has done (II Cor. 5:10). Scripture also warns us that there will be some surprises on that day. Some who have thought themselves to be saved will be disowned by the Lord. And others, who have doubted themselves (but trusted in Christ) will be given a blessed reward (Matt. 7:21-46). But *all* who have been justified, adopted, and sanctified in Christ will be openly acknowledged and acquitted by Him. That is, the Lord himself will declare that they are His, and that they are accepted in His sight, because they have found their righteousness in Him alone. It is true, of course, that men will be "judged every man according to their works" (Rev. 20:13). But this does *not* mean that any will be saved on account of anything that they themselves have done. The Bible clearly says that no man is saved because of his own good works. It is by faith in Jesus Christ only that any man can be saved. But the only kind of faith that really is saving, is the kind of faith that produces good works. "Faith without works is dead" (James 2:26). The good works come into consideration on judgment day, then, only as evidence of faith. Those who have *no* good works

157

to show will thus have no way to pretend that they have faith. And all who do have good works—however "small" they may be—will be justified in their claim that they do believe.

There will be different rewards for different people on that great day. But all—from the least to the greatest—will be "made perfectly blessed in the full enjoying of God to all eternity." And even that believer who receives the "least" reward will count himself rich beyond all imagination, and will rejoice with the man whose reward is greatest. There will no longer be such a thing as envy in the hearts of God's children then. But most of all we need to remember that all the saved will have God himself. This is the ultimate reward. For, as the Psalmist said, "in *thy presence* is fulness of joy: at thy right hand there are pleasures for evermore" (Ps. 16:11). We sometimes think of "heaven" as if the thing that made it so wonderful was the joy of seeing certain people who have "gone on before." But the Bible says that *God* is the believer's exceeding great reward (Gen 15:1). And when that day comes, the believer will realize as never before that the "heaven" of heaven is the "full enjoying of God to all eternity." Then will man at last reach his "chief end" which is "to glorify God, and to enjoy Him forever."

Questions:

1. What is meant by "resurrection"?
2. Why is this said to be unbelievable today?
3. Are these "difficulties" really new? Prove.
4. Why did the Apostles believe this doctrine?
5. Did Paul explain how God could, or would, raise the dead? Why?
6. Where does Paul give us some assistance in understanding the resurrection?
7. What other illustrations might be given?
8. In the picture we have another illustration not discussed in the text. In your own words show how it illustrates the resurrection body.
9. What are the two important points to remember concerning the resurrection body?
10. What will happen on the last day? (List as many things as you can from memory, then check yourself.)
11. What will be the criterion of judgment (the test by which men are judged)?
12. Does this imply salvation by works? Explain.
13. Will all receive the same reward? Why? Will all receive God?
14. What do some people desire as the great reward? Why is this wrong?

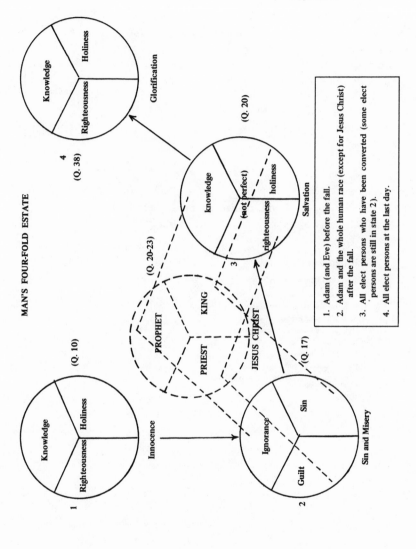

Appendix A

MAN'S FOUR-FOLD ESTATE

1. Adam (and Eve) before the fall.
2. Adam and the whole human race (except for Jesus Christ) after the fall.
3. All elect persons who have been converted (some elect persons are still in state 2).
4. All elect persons at the last day.

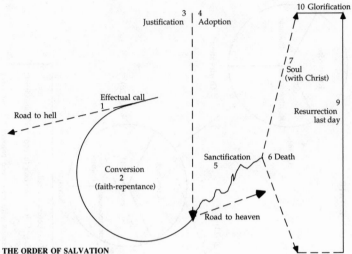

Road to hell

Effectual call
1

Conversion
2
(faith-repentance)

3   4
Justification | Adoption

Sanctification
5

6 Death

Road to heaven

10 Glorification

7
Soul
(with Christ)

9
Resurrection
last day

THE ORDER OF SALVATION

A man is walking down the road to hell.

1. He is effectually called.

2. He is converted (by faith and repentance).

3., 4. He is instantly justified and adopted.

5. He is gradually sanctified, during the rest of his life.

6. He dies.

7. His soul goes to heaven.

8. His body enters the grave.

9. At the resurrection of the last day, body and soul
together enter into

10. Glory.

KINDS OF RELIGION

	TRUE	MIXED	FALSE
(T) **TOTAL DEPRAVITY**	- MAN IS EVIL IN EVERY PART - CAN DO NOTHING TO SAVE HIMSELF	- MAN IS PARTLY EVIL - CAN DO SOMETHING TO HELP SAVE HIMSELF	- MAN IS GOOD - CAN DO EVERYTHING TO SAVE HIMSELF
(U) **UNCONDITIONAL ELECTION**	- ALL MEN DESERVE NO MERCY - GOD HAS CHOSEN SOME	- ALL MEN DESERVE SOME MERCY - GOD CHOOSES THOSE WHO CHOOSE HIM	- ALL MEN DESERVE MUCH MERCY - EVERY MAN CHOOSES HIS OWN DESTINY
(L) **LIMITED ATONEMENT**	- CHRIST DIED TO MAKE SALVATION CERTAIN FOR SOME	- CHRIST DIED TO MAKE SALVATION POSSIBLE FOR ALL	- CHRIST DIED TO SET AN EXAMPLE
(I) **IRRESISTIBLE GRACE**	- HOLY SPIRIT GIVEN TO SOME - HE ENABLES THEM TO REPENT, BELIEVE	- HOLY SPIRIT GIVEN TO ALL - HE HELPS THE ONES WILLING TO CONVERT	- HOLY SPIRIT NOT NEEDED - MEN CAN CHANGE THEMSELVES
(P) **PERSEVERANCE OF SAINTS**	- GOD KEEPS HIS ELECT FROM FALLING - THEY WILL NEVER FALL	- GOD HELPS ALL WHO COOPERATE - THEY MAY, OR MAY NOT, FALL	- MEN MUST KEEP THEM-SELVES - THEY CAN KEEP THEM-SELVES